The Sacred Cows Are Dying

ALSO BY ART GREER

No Grown-Ups in Heaven

The Sacred Cows Are Dying

Exploding the Myths We Try to Live By

Art Greer

HAWTHORN BOOKS, INC.

Publishers/New York

A Howard & Wyndham Company

ST. PHILIP'S COLLEGE LIBRARY

THE SACRED COWS ARE DYING

Copyright © 1978 by Art Greer. Copyright under International and Pan-American Copyright Coventions. All rights reserved, including the right to reproduce this book or portions thereof in any form, except for the inclusion of brief quotations in a review. All inquiries should be addressed to Hawthorn Books, Inc., 260 Madison Avenue, New York, New York 10016. This book was manufactured in the United States of America and published simultaneously in Canada by Prentice-Hall of Canada, Limited, 1870 Birchmount Road, Scarborough, Ontario.

Library of Congress Catalog Card Number: 77-70123

ISBN: 0-8015-6509-X

2 3 4 5 6 7 8 9 10

To Art Greer, Sr.,
  who taught me to love the past

and

To Edna Bornefeld Greer,
  who taught me to stay ready for the future

085695

Contents

The
Sacred
Cows
Are
Dying

1

No Wonder My Anchor Is Floating!

EVERYTHING WORKS OUT FOR THE BEST

If everything works out for the best, I could drink hydrochloric acid and get good results. Everything eventually works out, and probably in the *long* run, for the best, but I've had many experiences that worked out for the "not-at-all-good." I've added two and two and come up with two and one-third, losing almost as much as I'd gained. Let me give an example of this kind of disappointment.

Sam Fangschleister decides to gamble the family fortune on National Buggy Whip stock and loses it. He then must go to work as a ditchdigger and learns a lesson. How is that for the best? Maybe the truism isn't all that true! That's a frightening thought. We are surrounded by truisms, slogans, clichés, mottoes and other Stone Tablets that everyone "knows" to be true. What if they're all not quite true? It's important to know. Following a guideline that misleads us can really be disastrous.

And there are so many slogans: "A penny saved is a penny earned"; "Early to bed, early to rise . . . "; "The family that prays together, stays together"; "A stitch in time saves nine"; "If at first you don't succeed . . . "; "Do unto others . . . "; "Everything comes to him who waits." With all these pieces of

3

ST. PHILIP'S COLLEGE LIBRARY

wisdom, you'd think we would all be making hay while the sun shines and loving every minute of our lives.

Someone said, "You shall know the truth and the truth shall set you free." I think that's usually true. The clearer my insights, the easier it is to deal with life. Each time I find some truth, I know what to do with it. My problem is how to find truth in this plethora of maxims and mottoes, all of which sound so good. It is especially tough work when they conflict, like "Haste makes waste" and "He who hesitates is lost." So many of them preach beautifully. It's a reasonably dull person who can't write a fine, inspirational, five-minute talk about saving money. The trick is getting a slogan to work when it's tried! I'd rather not have a "true saying" if I can't make it work for me, because if it doesn't, I end up feeling worse! I would know how to act but still not have the desired outcome!

Slogans and mottoes (like buzz saws) are very useful, but only if they are true *and* applicable and if we know how to use them. Otherwise they can be downright dangerous.

In this chapter I will look at how we got the mottoes in the first place and why a lot of them aren't working any longer. During the rest of the book I'll be dealing with ten of the "biggies" that I think are leading people astray.

How did we get all these slogans? They must be useful or we wouldn't keep them around! Mottoes and "true sayings" have their origin in how we have learned to deal with our world, but there are *two* kinds of "reality" in our world. The first is the actual Stuff of the universe—chairs, people, words, events. The second "reality," which is just as real, is the structure one puts on that Stuff. I form this structure by my perception, and by my interpretation, of what I experience. Both of these "realities" are based on what I have come to call a *Conceptual Grid*.

All of us view our world through a set of concepts. From almost our first days of life we begin to wire up our brains in a very particular sort of way. "I like this." "That hurts." "This tastes better than that." By the time we reach six or seven our concepts are more sophisticated. "Good people do this." "People should obey their elders." "I'll never amount to much." When assembled, these pieces form what I see as a conceptual set of Polaroid glasses—a Conceptual Grid—a way of seeing Life.

Have you ever looked through two pieces of Polaroid glass? When the polarizing crystals in both pieces are parallel, a lot of light shines through, but turn one of the lenses 90° to the other, and *all* light is blocked. The point of this experiment is to show that each lens is blocking some light while letting other rays pass through.

The Conceptual Grids in our heads are like that. Each value decision we make determines the structure we are going to lay on the Stuff or reality out there. This is an important process. The reality of the external world must be structured internally before we can successfully deal with it. Our Conceptual Grid defines and structures our external world, limiting it in the process, so we are not overwhelmed by the ten billion things available to us. So we decide, "That isn't worth my time." "I won't do that." Piece by piece we pick out which part of the external world we choose to live in.

Unfortunately, to the degree that our Conceptual Grid is inaccurate (and doesn't fit the external world) it distorts the external reality. I heard a cute example the other day; a four-year-old, watching his mother drive the car, finally figured out something. "I know how you know where to go!" he smiled. "Those *lights* (pointing to the turn indicator) tell you which way to turn!" Little kids work hard at figuring out their world, trying to make some sense out of all that data.

I remember the terrible time I had in the third grade, I think it was. I was hard of hearing back then, and also doing a lot of Staying Home Sick. For one reason or the other, I missed the lesson when the teacher told us how to tell a paragraph when we saw one. When, one day, she started asking us to "read the next paragraph," I broke out in a cold sweat and started some Fast Figuring. I wasn't about to *ask*! I didn't want to watch the kids snicker and pass notes again about how old Dumb-arse missed another one. In a controlled panic, praying she wouldn't call on me before I figured it out, I noticed that the other kids always stopped reading when the words ended before the right-hand margin. Whew! Prayer worked! About a minute later she called on me and I set off with great confidence. There was only one problem—the last line of *my* paragraph ran right smack into the margin, so I kept on reading. I avoided neither the Dumb-arse title nor the titters. My Conceptual Grid had failed me because it distorted reality.

Want to see how it happens? In the figure above, you see the Roman numeral "9." Your task, should you choose to do it, is to draw one line and change it into a "6." (No fair peeking!) Did you figure it out? I spent a long time getting the wrong answer. For the secret, see the upside-down footnote.* If you had trouble, it was because I deliberately messed with your Conceptual Grid. By calling the figure a Roman numeral, I invited you to believe the answer would also be one, and helped you ignore the fact that two-thirds of the answer was staring you in the face.

Most of my problems are based on the same misperception. Have you ever had the experience of waiting for a red light,

---

*Put a curved line (the letter "S") before the "IX."

and out of the side of your eye seen the car next to you slowly moving forward? With just the right angle of vision, it seems as if *it* is standing still while *you're* moving! That's happened to me a few times. Each time I almost ruined my brakes trying to get my already-still car stopped! My perception changed my "reality."

In working through personal problems, one of the hardest lessons to learn is that we impose our reality on the Stuff around us. Frequently, our interpretations and perceptions are accurate. Just as frequently they are not. When I first landed in Turkey, I believed the Turks to be extremely un-friendly. I made that decision by observing their faces, most of which were grim, and somehow even grimmer when they looked at me. They didn't smile at each other. Their conversa-tions were terse. I didn't experience any "warmth." But sur-prise, surprise! The first time I threw out a "Merhaba! Nasilsunez?" to one of them, he exuded friendliness. The Turks weren't unfriendly—they were waiting for an "Hello, how are you?" from me. My Conceptual Grid had been cer-tain that "friendly people" smiled and talked a lot (and usually first).

Our Conceptual Grids tell us what's good or bad for us, whom to hang around, what to do with our time, what kind of furniture to buy, and the books we should read. It influences our sex lives, our professional lives, our free time, our sports, and our choices of food. We don't come by all that informa-tion easily.

Eric Berne, the founder of Transactional Analysis, postu-lated that each person has a complete network of feelings, thoughts, and behaviors that informs his Conceptual Grid. He called this the Parent Ego State. It is composed of some twenty-five thousand hours of input, mostly "wired together" in our heads by the time we are six or seven. In this network we have stored all the information we obtained from our parents and other big people concerning *their* Conceptual Grids. Our Parent Ego State defines our world for us and remembers all the mottoes and slogans. It sends out a multitude of messages, from "Ladies should keep their legs crossed" to "Boys should not cry." The messages cover a range from "You don't really have to do this but you should" to "If you don't do this you will really be in trouble!"

Our families gave us these principles, but most of them were operating in our families because the neighborhood and the community believed them to be true. The opinions and values and concepts of the society around us had a massive impact on what we learned was "true." In T.A. (Transactional Analysis) we refer to this larger social force as the Cultural Parent.

Each neighborhood, each city, each country has its own set of values and a pile of mottoes to support those values. We talk about our values as if they were universally true, but I suspect that few of them are "absolutes." One has only to visit first the North and then the South of the United States or Italy or France or Germany to become aware that more than the costumes are different. The people think differently. Their values are not at all uniform. Their mottoes and slogans differ because their experiences have differed.

In America, we are shocked at the callousness with which many oriental cultures view life. Life seems cheap to them, and we are awed by their indifference. We spend millions of dollars and hours deciding whether or not the people in Utah can shoot a criminal, or whether a girl, long in a coma, can be taken off life-sustaining machinery: Yet we read that in the Orient, people die in the streets while passersby merely shrug their shoulders. Why? Perhaps it has something to do with living in a place where the rate of births is faster than that of deaths, so natural, accidental—or even deliberate—deaths are happy assistance to the problem of overpopulation and not disasters. The situations we experience create both our mottoes and our morality.

I'd like to point out that *everyone* is moral: Everyone has a set of perceptions and concepts with which he interprets life. When we refer to other persons as "immoral" we mean that they aren't following *our* set of rules! We call other people "amoral" and mean that we can't see them following any particular set. "Immoral" people break my rules. "Amoral" people won't even use my categories! Their morality may not be as well thought through as mine, although frequently it is. The point is that often they *do* have a morality, and it serves a purpose for them.

Forcing other people to accept our morality is immoral. (I'm aware that's my judgment, and it's based on my conviction that we all should be allowed to believe what we want to believe. How we choose to *act* is a different matter.) Example: When my religious forefathers went to "save" Hawaii, they quickly set about trying to change the ways of behaving and thinking among the inhabitants. Some of the things the natives did probably needed changing, like burying people alive under the foundations of new houses to drive away evil spirits. Basically, however, the Hawaiians had a fairly solid and useful morality. In the process of disrupting their set of rules, we gave them a lot of misery. (Read Michener's *Hawaii* and you'll see what I mean.)

Someone told me a delightful story about that process. One of the first things the Congregationalists wanted to do was to cover up all the naked female breasts. (Breasts have frequently reminded people of illegal sex and the temptation of the Devil. I wonder why they haven't reminded us of milk?) So the good brothers, apparently unable to concentrate on their Bibles, sent home a request for garments that looked like our T-shirts. When they were distributed to the women, the natives were ecstatic. Good idea! The women appeared the next morning with twin holes cut in the front of each garment. Being practical, it made no sense to them either to hinder the feeding of babies, or to block off the view of something so obviously nice to look at. (I think it served the missionaries right!)

Societies, like individuals, struggle for survival. What we call morality is nothing more than the society's consensus of what is important for survival. Once we have conquered that, however temporarily, we can afford to begin thinking about things like meaning and purpose—how to survive *well*. Our solutions will depend on our experiences, for morality is a matter of geography.

Moral issues are related to survival. We don't much care how people decorate the insides of their homes because that doesn't affect our survival. We do care if they throw their garbage out the kitchen window to rot, or drive recklessly, because those things affect our chances of living longer. When enough people begin to feel threatened, the group swings into "moral action."

Group opinions have a fantastic impact on our Conceptual Grids, especially when we are young. We will do almost anything to avoid being shamed. Eskimos teach four-year-old children to avoid thin ice by having a group shame them loudly when they approach this danger. The morality of the group is an attempt to bring some degree of stability into our lives, and so we make a moral issue out of anything that appears to threaten the length or quality of our survival.

The same is true for our individual moral code. Each of us, consciously or not, has put together and continually reworks a network of things we consider valuable to our survival and well-being. Given our experiences, we do the best we can. I have long believed that at any moment in time we each live as well as we know how to. When we behave less well than we'd like, it's because we cannot figure out how to do better in that particular situation.

As we stabilize our lives, we raise up mottoes and slogans that seem to work for us. The deeper the conviction, the bigger the banner. The more people who approve, the bolder and "truer" the statement. The statements come in three varieties: a) *Stone Tablets,* on which God His Very Self has printed the motto: "By the sweat of thy brow shalt thou earn thy bread"; b) *God didn't say it, but we all know it's true:* "It's a dog-eat-dog world out there"; and c) *those we can't prove, but which would make a nicer world if everyone would act on them.* "People should be more understanding."

So long as the world is stable, these mottoes, sayings and slogans work well. They are guidelines to put order into our lives. They serve as compasses with which we can get a "fix" on what's happening. If I want to sail to South America I can lay a ruler to the chart and discover that I need to head, say, east by my compass—from Houston. As the seas and winds push me in different directions, I can return east by my compass and know that I'm back on course. Our cultural truisms serve as a steady point to steer by.

Unfortunately, the world and its people do not stay constant. Events force us to change the values and concepts by which we live. These events push "our little boats" well off course, much as a hurricane might leave a vessel a hundred miles south of where the captain intended it to be. Now the compass setting of east is no longer useful. To follow that old heading leads to an unnecessarily long journey and sometimes disaster. The destination remains the same, but the direction needs to be altered. A new heading of northeast (or maybe north) is now the right heading.

When the world came crashing out of the Dark Ages into the Middle Ages, it was a time of enormous social change. While many factors were involved, the one that scholars agree was the *major* factor was Gutenberg's invention of movable type for the printing press. Books now were available to the common man. No longer were priests the only ones who could read the Bible—Joe and Shirley Shoemaker could read it for themselves and make their own judgments about The Word. New ideas quickly passed around the continent, and with that, incredible changes began to take place.

In our time, World War II served as just such a catalyst and produced a multitude of social changes. For example, women from the hills of Kentucky came to Indiana to work at "the shipyard." They earned in a week more money than their families had received for months of hard labor before the war. I once watched two such women standing at a jewelry counter. One turned to the other and complained, "Help me pick something, Josephine. I've still got $10 and today is payday." Coming from a close-with-money family, I went into shock and apparently have never forgotten the conversation. With the war came movement, and with movement came moral change.

The charges wrought by that war alone would have entailed twenty years' work getting back on course. However, we also experienced the shock of an almost unbelievable advance in scientific and technological skills. Within a twenty-year period, four things happened that have since had greater impacts than even Gutenberg's printing press.* Nuclear power has increased the strength of our muscles and our capabilities. Television has increased the distance mankind can *see* (after its invention, for the first time, we could watch events happening on the other side of the city or the world). The computer expanded our "mind" a thousand times. We can now do things in an hour that would have taken five hundred people a hundred years to accomplish. Finally, the invention of the birth control pill has drastically affected the way people relate to each other sexually, and influenced the reproductive morality of many cultures.

---

*This is a thesis of Marshall McCluhan.

I am quite prepared to believe that we are both enjoying and suffering the consequences of having gone through four simultaneous renaissances. Alvin Toffler deals with these changes in his book, *Future Shock.* Not only the number of changes, but the very *rate of change,* are increasing almost faster than we can handle. The shock waves of our Quadruple Renaissance have blown us "hundreds of miles off our previous course." I think it is crucial to recognize and admit to this rapidity of change.

When I was a kid, I knew the brand, model, and year of every car on the road. No big deal; there were only a dozen types or so. Once you got the idea of a Buick you could spot one a mile off. Each brand came in three grades—plush, comfortable, and something-to-get-you-there. Chrome, or lack of it, was how you could tell the differences. Now there are dozens and dozens of brands. What used to be Chevrolet now comes in seven different brands! Some of these come in two or three styles like hatchback or notchback. Some come with a choice of three or four different engines. Even after you've decided on a basic brand you still have a hundred decisions to make before you even know what kind you want. You have to decide issues such as color, radio, airconditioning, shifting, and so on. We suffer from Over-Choice today. Remember when you could decide that you wanted a pair of blue jeans? There was *one* kind. Now. . . .

The point is, the life-style of our community has changed with the world. That means we have to change our guidelines from time to time. Hanging onto decisions we once made, but that are inappropriate for today's world, is as crazy as keeping a small sports car, if it's the only car you have, after the fourth kid is born.

You cannot get to your destination from where you are supposed to be or from where you were! It is relatively easy to figure out how to get from here to there, even when there are obstacles. What I find difficult is trying to get from the kitchen to the front door when I think I'm in the bedroom! I will carefully walk "around the bed" and fall into the sink. Now I'm really confused. I "know" I'm in the bedroom because it's two o'clock in the morning! Who moved the sink into my bedroom? Why is the world so bewildering?

I see people trying to solve their problems on the assumption (or the pretense) that they are where they were, or are supposed to be. "Of course I like my job; I'm a lawyer!" "Of course I enjoy being with my mate." "Of course reading this kind of book helps my mind." "Of course I care for other people." "No, money isn't the most important thing for me." "No, I'm not angry with you." And so on.

Many families have wrestled long and hard with the fact that the Family Supper Time is quickly becoming an occasional thing. The old rules were clear—families were supposed to have one meal a day together. Now, dad gets home after two of the kids have left for their functions, another isn't back yet from baby-sitting, and mom is on *her* way to night school at the local university. Let's try again Saturday.

A Houston pastor* described his problem with changing values this way:

> I was programmed as a boy to the value that one strong measure of a man was that he sacrificed to support his family. . . . I did not understand how deeply programmed was the value of being a sacrificially good provider. The implication in that value, of course, is that *paterfamilias* will be rewarded with gratitude from his family. . . . In sum, that value programmed into me as a boy . . . has become suddenly obsolete, at least in my life situation right now. My reaction, before I came to see what was happening, was anger. So that value by which I

---

*the Reverend Webster Kitchell

judged myself a good man has brought me shame and anger, in large measure through circumstances which were beyond my control. . . . Now I am in a new life situation, and to preserve my sanity I have to give up some old values. I am not sure how I will judge myself in the years ahead, but I am suddenly much more content and once again self-confident.

The old slogans and mottoes worked yesterday (if they did) when the world's experience supported them. Today, many of them no longer shed light on our experience. "Old sayings" should shed light on the path ahead; when they cease shedding light, they are worthless. No light is shed through mere continual repetition of worn-out words and clichés. A guideline works for me when I'm clear about what it means, how it will look when I use it, and what happens for the better when I do. Otherwise it's just another phrase that "people say."

Before we move on to the next Old Timer, I'd like to comment on the issue of losing our moral fiber. We have a "Letters to the Editor" column in our daily paper. Reading these letters is a good way to stay in touch with what the Hysterical People are thinking. (The letters *sound* hysterical.) One of the more popular issues is "losing our moral fiber." Some folk decide we are LOMF *every* time morality changes. I don't think so. We are dealing with *change*, not necessarily a lessening of principle. Given the fantastic changes that are occurring around us, it seems appropriate that we adjust our compass headings to fit each new situation. The readjustments won't always be right the first time.

The men who fought at Concord bridge back in 1775 are now spoken of as men fighting for such great issues as democracy, motherhood, and the right to bear credit cards. *They* clearly understood that they fought to prevent the British from burning down their barns! A lot of them didn't know anything about Parliament—they were simply protecting their homes.

Since Vietnam, many people have refused to fight "just any old war" unless their homes or loved ones were clearly in danger. There has been no lessening of moral fiber, but surely a lot of change.

All this is by way of saying that if you are struggling with morality, with your values, with your "goods and bads," then you are acting appropriately. You don't need to feel bad about that.

2
Won't Somebody Please Like Me

LOVE ME, LOVE MY DOG!

Do you remember the last time you trotted your new boy-friend or girlfriend out before the public? Junior prom, cocktail party, whatever. The first chance you got to be alone with someone from your in-group you may have asked, "Well, Charlie, what do you think of her?" or "Shirley, isn't he just the most perfect . . . ?" "Do you think he talks too loud?" "She isn't too tall, is she?" You wanted something fierce to know how they saw your new friend.

Why in the world would you want to know? What possible difference would it make what "they" thought? *You* were the one who was going to have to spend time with the person under scrutiny. The only really important opinion was yours, and yet you wanted to know what "they" thought.

There is a small, but very strong and determined, part of our personality which never sees itself as separate from the rest of the world. If we find *any* connection between us and another object or person, then it is experienced as "part of us." For example, can you picture yourself saying to some friends, "We'd like you to come over for dinner and bridge because we adore being with you beyond belief. We enjoy everything about

17

you—well, with one exception. Will you please not bring your kids because we can't stand the little perishers?" No. Only a clod or the latest graduate from the Let-It-All-Hang-Out-School would dare be that honest. Why? Because 87.3 percent of the parents in the world see their children as an absolute extension of themselves both physically and emotionally. If you want to be with them, you have to at least *act* as if you think their kids are pretty wonderful, too. Wouldn't you like to have a dollar for every friendship you've seen busted up because of "the kids"?

Children are just the beginning. Probably the next step is their home and the interior thereof. Unless your friends are fairly healthy, put-together people, you probably won't want to tell them that their latest painting doesn't at all speak to you of "the silence of eternity impinging on man's uncertainty." Be more explicit ("No, it looks more as if the artist were cleaning out his brushes on a bath towel") and you will find yourself treading water in fifty-thousand fathoms of hostile and unbelieving glares. If you're going to "not like" a part of their home, you had better make it sound as if something is missing in your cultural background. Their home is seen as an extension of *them*, like the kids.

Same with the family pet. You'd better think their German shepherd, Heinrich, is pretty clever to pin your shoulders to the couch that way, especially if *they* think that's cute. He's part of them, too. In fact, that's where one of our Big Mottoes comes in—"Love me, love my dog!" It's a package deal.

You don't hear this motto said out loud much. But I surely see it followed a lot. While most of us "know better," we still want (with all our heart) and expect other people to be awestruck with our choice of lover, impressed beyond belief by our children, amazed at our good taste in home and surroundings, green with envy at our sporting equipment, entranced by our clothes, captivated by our choice of automobiles, and jealous of our jobs. Not to mention. . . .

If *we* like it, too, that's nice: but the most important thing is that "they" like it. If "they" *don't* like it, we are greatly distressed. I'm convinced that we seldom buy something simply because *we* like it. Mirrors are put in haberdasheries and boutiques so you can see how you look to others *out there!* That's what I want to know when *I* buy a suit.

If we were buying for our own pleasure, we would pay attention to how the clothing felt on us and how convenient the pockets were. As a result of the counterculture movement, many people are doing just that: wearing clothes-for-convenience (and do they ever look funny!). The minute we care "how we look" we are buying to please others.

I recall seeing an old duffer in Wichita Falls who drove a car that was sturdy but what my people would call "a disgrace." So were his overalls and shoes. I found out he was one of the richest men in Texas. The poor have to dress that way. The rest of us feel that our clothes are an extension of ourselves, and so we wouldn't dare dress like bums. That rich guy understood that everybody knew he was wealthy! He could dress any way he liked—he could "buy 'em and sell 'em," as we say in Texas.

This "love me, love my whatever" operation influences a good many of our dealings in life. If I want to eat cold, mashed potatoes late at night, I want everyone else to agree that my choice makes undeniable sense. If people do not agree, if they laugh at my choice of time schedule or end tables or an I-didn't-mean-for-that-to-be-funny remark, my first response is to begin to explain.

Explanations come in three varieties. Parents explain to children, "This is why you have to eat your spinach." And sometimes we explain how things work, such as information on how to wind a clock or shoot a gun. Most explanations are neither of the above, but rather a *defense*. "This is why I did that (and won't you please understand and agree with me)." We always had to explain what we did when we were little, and we never seem to get over it. "Well, the reason I was late was. . . ." Have you noticed that many people even have to announce their departure for the bathroom? Explaining their absence in advance! We have a gut feeling that if we can somehow sell the explanation, something really bad can be avoided. When a group laughs at my funny hat (which I think is quite serious), it doesn't mean that I'm a boob, or that the members of it are in the process of terminating their friendship. It means that they find my hat amusing: but the part of me that is only four years old *thinks they are going to go away, or downgrade me.* The explanations are an unnecessary attempt to keep those two disappointments from happening.

The conviction that if others really love us they will also love everything about us is *pervasive!* Believing it, we use everything in our world as a test of our worth. If someone I know doesn't like cold navy beans, it becomes a Big Deal and must be settled immediately, since I *do* like them. If you don't like what I like, then somehow you must not like me. If you think I'm raising my kids "wrong," we must have another battle (or at least some bad feelings). Being accepted seems to depend on every person we meet and most of the statements they make. If that is true, then we must spend our lives between a rock and a hard place! Life will hurt! And for most of us, it will. Nine out of ten people seem to spend their lives in just such a "stuck" position. Each encounter with another human becomes a test of self-worth and validity. Even encounters with pets! Remember the last time you wanted to pet a dog and he snapped at you? Bad feelings rise quickly in the not-yet-acceptable person when she feels that even a gentle, furry dog is saying go away!

Those who accept the fact that some people will never like them are rare indeed. They are even rarer if they decide it's OK for others not to! Most of us learned by the time we were six that our survival depended on pleasing mom and dad and the older kids. If the Big People got crabby, they *might* go away. How would we be fed then? Unless we work at it, that fear of abandonment never leaves. We learned at six that people were watching and judging us, and it was serious business. "John, when you do that I could kill you!" "Sally, your noise is driving me crazy!" "If you do that one more time, I'll never speak to you again." Parents say things like that without realizing that such exaggerated phrases are heard *literally* by a four-year-old, who can't yet think in general or abstract terms.

Slowly we come to understand, wrongly, that not only our worth and value but our very survival depends on other people and whether or not they approve of everything we do. "Sammy, you're bothering me again!" Does that mean he doesn't like me anymore? Does that mean she'll go away and leave me? Life is apparently either a "one up" or a "one-down" operation. One feels if he does something displeasing to another, either he is wrong (or "bad," or "unworthy," or "in danger") or the others are. Each encounter, then, becomes a football game, and the goal is approval.

We not only expect the contest to happen, but we *seek* it. It will prove either that we're acceptable as persons or that we will never be acceptable except in special ways. Listen to the conversations around you and to your own. Frequently you can hear a subtle, second message being sent. "Please notice what I'm doing (or what I did), approve of it, and tell me I am cute! Tell me I'm doing it right so I can feel worthy of you."

For many, life is an endless series of tap dancing steps designed to validate the right to be alive. I have termed this the "search for the superstroke," the Big Report Card that will say we have it all put together for once. Our quest for the *super-*

stroke means reaching perfection by everyone else's standards. That's why we dress "for other people." That's why we want other people to like our kids and home and cars—to be valid! And the goal is to become Good Old Boys whose mere presence evokes cries of "Wow! Isn't he a sweetheart!"

When 100 percent approval is the least you will settle for, *any* shortcoming is serious business. "It was a good report, but I didn't work on it long enough." "Yes, 749 people thought my sermon was magnificent, but one guy *didn't*. Oh, my God!" "My home is lovely, but the good ones are farther out." "Shirley gets fine grades, but she got a C in Chemistry." BLOTCHES! If you can't stand blotches, the only other choice is to get others to say "That isn't a blotch!" or fight them if they won't. Constantly. In my opinion, 98.3 percent of all fights and spats are *really* built on the foundation of "you don't love my dog, so you don't love me." I have to be right or I'm *alone!*

This is further complicated by our Conceptual Grids. As I search for approval, I do so with my "special way of looking at things" strapped firmly to my inner eye, and my "special way of thinking about the things I think I saw" serving as a computer. Put together, all of this forms a Road Map* to guide me on my journey. Let me illustrate how that works. If the people in my childhood family didn't like to get too close to each other, then a major highway got laid down on my Map. "It is wrong to get too close to other people." This general idea was then defined: "Here's what being too close looks like." Given that decision and that concept, I am now ready to pass judgment on myself and those around me. "They are dangerously close to each other; they're getting it all wrong. Bad things will happen!" The people being judged may not, in fact, be at all close, but I will *see* them as *too* close.

---

*Eric Berne called this a Script. "Scripting" and "programmed" are words that make people feel doomed. I prefer Road Map since it clarifies the issue. If my Map is inaccurate I can change it.

I've illustrated *one* such possible highway on our Life Road Map. Each of us has literally *thousands* of them. Based on our experiences, we "know" the Map is accurate. (Unfortunately, we don't know about our blind spots. I once said jokingly to a friend, "I don't have any blind spots; I looked and there weren't any!" Some folk say that seriously.) Thus equipped, we then march into the day's journey *expecting* to find that real life will conform to our Map. One of the first expectations we have is that other people will have had the same experiences of reality and therefore the same Map.

Air force navigator friends tell me that the worst thing a pilot can do while navigating is to force the ground beneath him to conform to his map. It is also the first thing most new pilots do! "There's supposed to be a river down there now—yeah, there's one, that'll do!" (It's actually a creek!) If the pilot continues to make the reality beneath him fit the reality of his map, he'll end up quite lost. The purpose of a map is to shed light on the territory surrounding us.

Our Conceptual Grids, or Life Road Maps, can shed light on what we experience. Unfortunately, most of us use the Map to *describe* the reality. Worse yet, we can insist that reality is what our Map says it is, and if we do, we will end up like the pilot, lost. People used to tell me (coming off their Road Maps), "You don't look or act like a clergyman." That sounded as if there were a list of requirements somewhere that universally fit the category. An accurate statement might have been, "You don't act like most clergymen," or "You don't act like any clergyman I've met before." But if a person *is* one, he or she will act like one, necessarily! We find out how engineers act by watching engineers. That isn't what we usually do, though.

More typically, we look at our Map and then put our expectations on the world. One clue to such expectations are sentences that begin with the words "It's only natural to. . . ." I, for example, think that Right-Minded People Always Fight Fair with People They Like, and I really get exercised when people insist on fighting "dirty." (I've got a long list of what "dirty" is, too!) I *expect* people to fight fairly, even though the evidence is that most of us *don't* fight that way. When we expect something contrary to the evidence, we get no better results than if we were to expect elevators to move sideways.

I'm thinking of some of the other ways I set myself up for "disappointments." I expect my light bulbs to burn forever; I expect merchants never to make billing errors; I expect my paper to be delivered every day and promptly; I expect people to be understanding and sensitive about what I do; I expect people to know that I am never angry when I yell; the list goes on and on. Do you have expectations that set you up, like expecting your loved one to "only have eyes for you?" Or that other folk will never be in a bad mood? Or that your employer will care at least as much for you as he does for making money?

Several "setup expectations" are corollaries to "love me, love my dog." "If you really love me you will. . . ," and "You are rejecting me when you say 'no' to me." If we expect that loved ones will always want to be around us or always like us or always approve of what we are doing at any given moment, we are setting ourselves up for sadness.

I would like to add still another piece to the puzzle of why we insist on using everything around us in our search for approval and a good self-image. It may also help parents who are struggling through the process of raising a two- or three-year-old child. Freud proposed—and subsequent research has shown—that we go through the first years of our lives in particular, discrete stages. During each one, a different part of our psyche, or personality, is formed, and he called these *developmental stages*. One occurs roughly between the ages of eighteen to thirty-six months. He called it the "anal stage." For personal and esthetic reasons, I will rename it the Stubborn Stage and describe it from the point of view of Transactional Analysis.

During the Stubborn Stage, we are involved in the task of separating ourselves from the world around us, particularly from mom. Up to then, she simply has been another part of ourselves. The child's big question during this period is, "Can I be me—can I be different from everyone else and still have my needs met? What happens if I should decide that today is Friday although the rest of the world wants it to be Tuesday? What happens if I say the ceiling is "down" and that grass is purple. Can I do that and still get away with it?

Good parenting at this stage requires that the child be allowed to be different so long as that difference doesn't physically harm him. The sharp dad will announce that "tomorrow will be Wednesday, except for Sherlock, for whom it will be Saturday." In such a healthy environment, the child will learn that he is allowed to be different and is a person in his own right. Having learned that, he will also soon discover that it is one helluva lot easier to go along with the world, especially when it comes to calendars.

You can appreciate how this can be fouled up if mom or dad is feeling insecure. "Oh, my God! I want him to be a lawyer and lawyers have to know what day it is. I must get him straightened out right this very minute!" This is the entrance transaction to the ongoing battle of the Terrible Twos. "It's Tuesday, Sherlock!" "Friday." "No, darling, you see, yesterday was Monday, wasn't it?" "No, yesterday was Wednesday and today is Friday." Seven transactions later, the parents are ready to weep with confusion and despair, and Sherlock is wondering why he can't be different. He doesn't care about the stupid calendar, but he desperately cares about being different.

If, according to their Life Road Map, parents are convinced

that they have to make their children "get it right every single time" if they want to make it through life, then their dealings with Stubborn Age children can be horrendous. (It's tough enough for parents who know what they are doing!) They will insist that their kid "get it right" and thereby teach him that it is not OK to be different. The child will never be able to separate himself emotionally from his parents. If development is impaired during this stage, we will continue to finish the job of separation as adults. We do that by being Contrary and Stubborn People.

We have all been around such folk. Remember the guy who is always angry? No matter what goes on around him, his response (or hers) is always "Rmmpf rrrmpf!" He's always tapped-off about something or other. I suspect we all have some discontent going on—anger that simply isn't appropriate to the situation. Do you know some folk who are still mad at God because the grass isn't colored fuschia? Do you know some who get *angry,* not just irritated, when the traffic signal turns red in front of them, or who are angry because there are other people in the world who *want to use the same freeway*? Freud called this "anal anger" as opposed to the "oral anger" which occurs when something such as food is taken away from us. A child feels "anal anger" when he is aware that the world doesn't revolve around him. That anger is a tool for helping him *feel* separate. It's as if the kid were saying, "Well, if the world won't do what I say, the least I can do is get outraged."

In this book I generally suggest another way of translating the motto or slogan under discussion, or at least another way of looking at it. I can't find an alternate way of looking at "Love me, love my dog," however. I believe this is purely a motto for Losers, and I can't think of a thing to recommend it. Trying to get 100 percent approval is programming for failure.

I'd like to conclude this chapter with three quick ideas which

I think are helpful to break loose from the perceived need to be Good Old Boys.

First, our best attempts at belonging 100 percent to a group—whether family, neighborhood, or club—will *never* successfully change the fact that we are single, solitary individuals. We talk about couples as if there were such a reality. (The reality is that two single people choose to be together in certain ways.) Couples frequently say "we" a lot because that word somehow helps push away the reality of each person's individuality. I am not discounting the things we do together, nor the importance of community. These are also real: but Togetherness does not preclude the fact that each of us is alone in a very real sense. It cannot be proven, for example, that the color you see when *you* look at the sky is the same color *I* see. We have merely agreed that whatever color each of us sees when we look at the sky will be called blue, and that works out fairly well. Accepting our singleness is the crucial first step toward understanding ourselves.

We are "ships that pass in the night," as the poet said. We will be in the same boat with others for only short periods of time. Given that fact, the question is how do we sail with each other? How can we best communicate? And with whom do we choose to sail this particular day?

Finally, what no one understands at age five (and few realize fifty years later) is that we *will* be liked and considered Good Old Boys by *somebody*, no matter what we do! The conviction that everyone will go away if we aren't "right" is simply not true. As I write this, a convicted murderer will be shot in two days. As he has waited out the legal battles involved in authorizing his execution, he has become a folk hero of strange proportions. His latest occupation has been responding to all the folk who have started writing to him as a "Dear Abby" consultant!

The question should be not "How do I get somebody to like

me," but "What sort of people do I want to like me?" Still better is, "What kind of person do I really want to be, and will I like the kind of people I will then attract?" That we might end up in life with no one around us is a fear no one takes lightly. Few of us find the role of hermit appealing for more than a short while. Transactional analysis has taught us that if scads of people do not find us worth being around, it is not because we *lack* something but because we are doing something to keep them away from us. We are working at it. In a world of three billion people, it is becoming increasingly difficult *not* to have people around us.

Demanding that people accept all of us or nothing ("Love me, love my dog") is a way of keeping people winnowed out, if that's what is wanted. There are easier, more comfortable ways of choosing not to be with folk.

It's OK to be different; OK because each of us *is* different and will always be so. People will still love us. Think a minute. Do you know someone who is *really* different—does things and wears things that others wouldn't dream of wearing or doing—and yet you find that person really attractive because of who he or she is?

One of my best friends never liked my dog—hated her, as a matter of fact (probably because the dog always wanted to bite my friend). It had nothing to do with me; it was a matter between my friend and Freckles. If I wanted to see much of my friend, I would make sure the dog wasn't around when he came to visit. I didn't have to kill either one, though, to keep from feeling "unacceptable."

3

Shape Up or Ship Out

YOU MUST BE PERFECT,
AS YOUR FATHER IN
HEAVEN IS PERFECT

If there is one thing we're *all* certain of, and have been since we were three years old, it's that we are supposed to Shape Up. We understand we aren't acting as we're supposed to, and that somebody has a list of laws and rules somewhere that describes how we will be when we Shape Up. Sometimes we also understand that no matter how hard we try, we probably won't make it. The big problem, then, is to fake it well enough so we won't have to Ship Out—pack up our gear and move away.

I'm not against some basic social regulations. I agree the "shape up or ship out" motto is appropriate when someone insists on treating the world as his or her ashtray, and the "rules of the house" say not to put your cigarettes out on the floor. Or, in another example, if you refuse to drive on the right side of the road, then I want you either to get out of the driver's seat or go to England where you'll just love driving on the left.

I appreciate most laws and rules. They are important for controlling harmful behavior. "Thou shalt not spit on the sidewalk and make thy neighbor sick." "Thou shalt not make holes in thy neighbor's body with little round lead objects."

"Thou shalt not dump thy garbage into thy neighbor's mess kit." Social laws are important. They keep us from bumping into each other. They reduce the stresses and strains of life. However, some rules make things worse and should be rescinded. Paul wrote that "the very commandment which promised life proved to be death to me." Another way of saying that: "Your rules aren't helping me, pal. They're killing me."

The problem with learning to Shape Up as children, however, was that while we were learning socially useful behaviors, we were fully aware that our very survival depended on "getting it right" and pleasing those we needed. I am convinced (with no way to document it) that we "know" in our muscles and flesh, if not in our brains, that if we don't get things "right" we could die. Why else would otherwise simple problems take on such mammoth proportions in our guts?

As children, we received information about how to survive in our family, our neighborhood. A lot of it was good, such as the admonition "Don't pull that boiling pot over." It was the *bad* information that hurt. "Work is better than nonwork, even when it is nonproductive." Or, "Do something, even if it's wrong!" Or, "If something is really fun, there must be something wrong with it!" (Equally harmful: "Eat, drink, and be merry, for tomorrow we die!" Some people do nothing but play while waiting for death.)

As we worked our way through the process of "getting it right" we were making many decisions about who others were, who we were, and how we were expected to act. One of the commonest decisions we reached was "I am never supposed to feel good about being who I *am*. I'm not supposed to feel what I feel, or think what I think. I'm supposed to be somebody else."

"See how nicely your sister is holding her fork, Sam?" (Damn, I got it wrong again!) "Why don't you get interested in football instead of stamp collecting, George?" (How come I like stamps instead of being "normal?") "Put down that hammer, Doreen. Girls like dolls, not woodworking." (What a tragedy; I'm really a boy in a girl's body.) "Don't be so emotional, Sarah Jean. Christian people control their emotions. Anger is the Devil working in you." (Guess so, but it sure *felt* like me!)

Since we were only little-bitty guys when we made these big decisions, we were in a pickle from the start. What to do? Look around, that's what. These big folk around us seem to be doing well. They're in such a good place that they even know how "impossible" we are. We'll watch what *they* do. And what do we see? *Onion Skins!** If you want to "make it," you have to find some onion skins and put them on, one by one.

Dad doesn't say, "Honey, I really feel depressed when I see all the trash piled in the corner. Will you help me carry it out?" He says, "Martha, ¢%#$%, it, you are the sloppiest woman in town. No wonder the kids are turning out the way they are." Perhaps it wasn't said so grossly at your house, but I'll bet something like that was said in socially acceptable, "sophisticated" ways. Already there's a piece of onion skin to use! "Never say what your position on an issue is; complain about the other guy. Get in the first lick when at all possible. The best defense is a good offense."

When we were children we saw that we could use our feelings to manipulate people. When mom got an answer from dad she didn't like, she went to a corner and pouted. Sometimes it took two days, but dad always gave in. He couldn't resist a pouter! When I tried pouting at dad, by golly, it worked! When dad wanted something from mom, he got angry. I tried

---

* "Onion Skins" is Fritz Perl's colorful analogy for the learned behavior we put on, a layer at a time. It hides the person underneath.

pulling an angry act on mom. Since she was really moved by anger, I learned another trick—to pout with dad and be angrily aggressive with mom. It didn't always work, but sometimes it did. *

Many of us learn to be passive to get what we need. Being assertive is tricky business in a family of Onion Skin wearers. Sometimes you have to assert yourself, but it is frequently quicker and more efficient to get someone else to do it for you. Waiting for others is a socially acceptable Onion Skin. "Tell me what to do, Charlie." (If he doesn't, I will wait for a better friend to come along.) "Are you using that ashtray?" (If he doesn't realize that I really want him to hand it to me, I'll put the ashes in my coffee cup.) "Sure would be nice to go out tonight." (Wait, wait; hope, hope.)

Another Onion Skin is "blaming it on others." "I can't have fun at parties because my wife is so reserved." "I can't be me because the company won't let me wear a turtleneck shirt." "My home is a riot because the kids won't shut up." "I'm not a neat person, all because my parents led me astray. (They switched my toilet seat when I was three; what do you expect of guy who had to go through that?)"

One last important Onion Skin to come! Taibi Kahler, a vibrant young transactional analyst, has identified five major concepts that "drive" people into bad places. We compulsively rely on these Drivers, thinking they are the key to an OK position in the world. We think we will become OK, or acceptable, if we are Perfect enough, Pleasing enough, Try Hard enough, are Strong enough or Hurry enough. Taibi says that all parental advice on "how to get it right" can be stuck in one of these five categories. We have all five of them, but for each of us one or two are primary. * *

---

*This is an example: The very *last* thing *my* mom would do is pout!
* *cf. T. Kahler and H. Capers, "The Miniscript," *TA Journal*, vol. 4:1, pp. 26ff.

Let me illustrate how these can get us into a "bad place." When I was working on a master's degree, my professor gave us an assignment. He made it clear that the format and procedures usually associated with academic life were of *no* interest to him. We could do the assignment at our leisure and commit our work to the back of an old envelope if we wanted. We could tape it or file it, and do with it as we wished. Whatever! He only wanted us to learn something from our work.

My personal Driver is *Hurry Up*. My gut impulse when in a crunch is to move faster. My favorite expressions have to do with "getting *on* with" the project at hand. I tend to move quickly. (I head immediately for the "bottom line," as businessmen say.) I'd much rather be done quickly than take time and do something *better*. I have to work at slowing down!

So I finished my assignment three days after he assigned it. No use hanging around! Fortunately, I spotted this as "dumb" and gave myself three more weeks to enjoy further work on the project for my own purposes. Another friend wanted to be Perfect and ruined his weeks there. He spent hundreds of hours in the library making sure each footnote was properly researched. He wrote and rewrote draft after draft. He spent the last week turning out flawless pages of typescript on the best bond paper available. The last night of our four-week stay, he came to my room about to flip out. He wasn't sure where the prof wanted the staples to go. Or should he use paper clips? Wow! He had missed a lot of things he had planned for himself by trying to be Perfect.

A person who had to be Strong would have insisted on reading thirty books and writing two hundred pages. She would also make sure that nothing personal showed in the finished product. A Pleaser would have spent a lot of time around the prof until he knew exactly what turned him on. Then he'd deliver that (probably on old envelopes, in this case). The Try Hard type would judge his performance on none of the above. The only thing that would count for him would be Good Old American Sweat.

Our Drivers push us into behavior that may not fit the situation. How would you like a brain surgeon with my Hurry Up? Or your accountant to be a Try Hard? ("I'll have your income tax done by June, Sam.") Some Be Perfects are married to Hurry Ups and they drive each other crazy.

One by one, the Onion Skins fall into place. We do accomplish some things with these learned behaviors, but at a very high cost in time and energy and bad feelings. More importantly, the Onion Skins reinforce our conviction that we're really *not* OK and probably won't ever be.

Even the Bible says so! The Good Shepherd himself said, "You must be perfect as your father in heaven is perfect"!

The folks have told me and told me. Hundreds of rules and regulations and musts and oughts and shoulds. Most of which I don't get right. Even my room is a mess. (Meaning my pattern of organization is different from everyone else's. I know exactly where everything is. What's a floor for if not to store things on?) I know I'm fouled up because nobody misses a chance to tell me when I go astray. From morning to night.

Then comes school. Not only are my behaviors monitored, but now they're going to work on my head! Gotta learn it. And in the "right" order. The other day I answered the question, "What do you think the poet meant by such-and-such a phrase" and I got it wrong. I suppose what the teacher wanted was for me to tell her what I thought she thought. It was bad enough to hear from the folks about my mess-ups, but now the kids go "shame, shame on Johnny."

The folks drag me to church. Don't much want to be there since I have absolutely no place to put the things they talk about. But while I'm trying to ignore what's going on, I can't help hearing more stuff about how what I think is bad. I'm sorry, but I just can't help staring at their breasts! I like to. Even if thinking about that is wrong. And I'm not supposed to resent Jimmy's dating the girl I like. And being angry at mom for making me wear these ridiculous shirts is wrong. And envying the class president. Why can't I sit around thinking about how good God is, like everyone else does?

College is pretty much the same, and so is working for the oil company. It's the same thing in spades. They have more expectations of what I'm supposed to look like than the military! I finally bought an expensive pen and pencil set the other day. They keep slipping as I write, but I'm sick of people snickering because I used a pen too cheap for "my position." I'd really like a smaller desk to work on — would love to have one of those little rolltops with pigeon holes. I'd work like crazy on one of those. But people in my grade use these damn things. Looks like the deck of an aircraft carrier. And I sure hope no one ever finds out how much I hate those stupid cocktail parties and flirting with a bunch of women I hardly know. God, I hope they don't discover that I'd rather be with Myrtle. Wonder what's wrong with me?

And the neighborhood I live in. Have to live there because my employer expects me to. The neighborhood knows what's "perfect," too. Like the grass; I can't stand cutting the stuff, but it comes with the house and if you don't keep it cut we'd be living in a jungle. Everybody says so. Tried to skip a week once and got a nasty note from Maynard. He and Kitty are really good at doing it right. They spend every weekend cutting grass. If I could just talk everyone into letting it grow, we'd all have permanently uniform lawns — about a foot up. Grass only grows so tall, you know. But Right Thinking People keep it at two inches. I'm screwed up again.

If that isn't enough, I get programs for "right living" from the Kiwanis, the PTA, the yacht club and good old Phi Beta Poo. The list is endless. If I were any good, I guess I'd like the furniture I have, I'd really get with gourmet eating instead of stick-

ing with the meat and potatoes I seem to enjoy so much, I'd work harder, and enjoy more, and enjoy football and hot dogs, and ice cream like everyone else. I wouldn't want to ride a motorcycle or spend so much time playing my guitar.

I'm supposed to be as perfect as God and I can't even get as perfect as my son who plays the clarinet better than I do! Fat chance I have of making it.

And so it goes with most of us. We are surrounded in many subtle ways (and some not so subtle) with banners that read: TRY HARD TO GET IT RIGHT, STUPID. Millions of folk are even flunking sex because they spend their time together "trying to get it right" according to the latest sexual-engineering manual. I wish I had a dollar for every white, middle-class couple who aren't allowed to enjoy sex unless they have simultaneous orgasms. "The Book" said so. (Sex isn't something you *do*. It's really something you *are!* Together, usually.)

With such instructions and "OKness as a Person" depending on nothing less than perfection, there are three choices. First, you can keep trying and not quite get there. Ever. Some time ago, a senior chaplain, explaining to new chaplains that the base commander was the real religious leader on any station, said that "if he wants a prayer service at 3 a.m. on top of the flagpole, you'd better be up there praying or covered with sweat trying to get there when three o'clock comes."

A lot of us decide that if we can't make perfection, we can at least try, so we keep aiming for it and failing. We fail, however, because there is always one person who isn't pleased with how we do it; there is always one little thing we forgot to do or did wrong; there always seems to be just a little more effort we could have produced. We could have done it sooner, or accomplished more. Thus we stay Losers in a world of Winners. Even if we win much, we're always Losers by somebody's standards.

A second, more common, way to react is to lower standards

so that we are "already perfect" and then spend our lives proving to the world that we *are*, by God, already perfect. It's *they* who are pretty much messed-up. "Floyd, you just work too many hours a day. You don't have time for gardening and book reading (like I do)." I think the main reason we make unnecessary problems for those around us is to reestablish some possibility that we are "without fault" and the trouble lies with others.

The only other choice in dealing with the TRY HARD TO GET IT RIGHT banners is to give up: It's a dumb world anyway. "Of course I'm not perfect. Nobody is. But what do you expect in such a totally fouled up world?" These people have really given in. Their answer to life is to surrender, but not without tossing a few critical looks at the rest of the world. If you point out that somebody seems well-balanced, they respond with something like, "Yeah? Well, I'll bet if the truth were known . . . "

What's so wrong about Trying Hard to be Perfect? Well, it doesn't make sense biologically, psychologically, intellectually, nor biblically. Since people tend to quote the Bible to prove that we don't amount to much and ought to try harder, I'd like to start there. (Sometimes they quote Shakespeare, mistaking a quote of his for the Bible.) If you're going to quote Bible passages, I think it is helpful to do it with accuracy and understanding. One of my goals is to wrestle the Bible back from those people who quote it the most, usually inaccurately, and use it to Shape Up the World according to their standards.

Our English phrase "You must be perfect" isn't an accurate translation of what The Man said. Jesus said something similar, but when it was written down in Greek the word was *teleios*. This doesn't mean "without fault" by any stretch of the imagination. Rather, it means "brought to completion; fully accomplished; fully developed; fully realized; complete; entire; WHOLE." The Greek noun from which this word comes means "fulfilling one's ultimate destiny," and has nothing to do with living an error-free life.

That makes it a whole new ballgame, doesn't it? Telling people they must "be without fault, like God Himself" is just one big joke. *Teleios* means being a whole, put-together, integrated person who functions on "all eight cylinders" instead of limping along on three or four. The Man was inviting us to make use of all our parts and all our potency instead of wasting ourselves in internal and external wars. The abundant life we want is not "out there somewhere" waiting to be claimed by the winners of the Get It Right contest. Neither is it something we'll find after we "get dead" and go to the Great Pot Luck Supper in the Sky. It's already inside us, hidden under a bushel of crazies—covered by our Onion Skins.

There's another line that used to bother me. "The Lord is my shepherd, I shall not want." Dang if I wasn't getting even *that* wrong! I want a lot of things, and it seems clear that if I were getting life right I wouldn't have any wants. I'd be patiently waiting for the Big Boss to deliver whatever seems right to Him. The line above has recently been retranslated by the American Bible Society to read, "The Lord is my shepherd; *I have all that I need.*" Now that makes sense! I already have all the equipment I need to get where I want to go. I don't have to wait until I get everything I want.

I hear a "gospel message" frequently on the radio, from the pulpit, and on distracting roadside signs. The idea in each is that we will only "get right with God" (suggesting you are one-down to start with!) if we succeed in killing a part of ourselves—under the guidance of their corrective action, of course.

Nonsense! The full life comes from "getting our act together." When we use all of the talents, all of the parts that we have, we become who we *are.* You have a right to be alive because you *are* alive. You are OK, which means that you have all the potential, capabilities, yearnings, needs, sensitivity, and energy that is available to every other creature on this planet. You make mistakes. Your mistakes usually cause you as much pain as they cause others, although perhaps in different forms and although you sometimes pretend not to hurt. Your needs are as valid as my needs. Your opinions are as important to you—if sometimes not as accurate—as others' are to them. You have a right to have your needs met. You have as much right to be wrong as other people. You have a right to your air space.

This is also true for the other guy.

I submit the last two paragraphs as a reasonably good definition of the much used and much misunderstood "I'm OK; You're OK." Jesus said it first (if that matters). You are important and I am important because we are both God's creation. We both fight the same battles, no matter how different they look on the surface. We are each unique individuals. Whether we like it or not, each of us is equally important to the universe. I think John Donne was right. "Ask not for whom the bell tolls; it tolls for thee." Whether we choose to notice it or not, the death of a brother or sister does diminish us. And we in turn are of equal importance, no matter what the other kids on the block said when we were little. We matter because we *are*.

Trying to prove we're OK is an endless, impossible task. We simply don't have the feedback. I preached a sermon once that was really a dog! It had a cute title, "Mental Albinos." Loved the title; hated the sermon. It didn't say anything, and I didn't say it well. Years later a woman approached me whom I didn't recognize. She asked me if I remembered preaching that sermon. Oh, boy, did I ever! I asked her why *she* remembered it. "I came to chapel that day to say 'goodbye.' I had intended to kill myself that afternoon. Something in that sermon changed my mind. Since then I've gotten my head straight and I'm really enjoying my life. I just wanted to say 'thank you.' "

Thank you? For what? For that dog of a sermon? Yep. It really *wasn't* much, and it certainly wasn't without fault, but it sure as heck was *perfect*—it did what it was intended to do by helping someone on her way.

I have a hammer in my work closet.* It's fairly well beat up. The handle has a lot of dents in it and some paint spots from being left out in the wrong place. The tip of one of the claws is busted off. Even the label bearing my name is now unreadable: but that hammer is a perfect hammer! It still does perfectly what it was designed to do.

What were you designed to do? For most of us it appears we were designed to do things other people picked out for us to do. If we want to do what we're designed to do, we have to start peeling off all the layers of Onion Skins we put there to accommodate other people and to defend ourselves.

By way of review, let me share the apt way my friend and colleague, John Bradshaw, lists our Onion Skins. He calls them the Five D's of Adaptation. We learn to *Defend*. "The reason I spilled the milk was because . . . " (meaning "see how I couldn't help it?"). We learn to *Defy*. "I don't have to take orders from you. You're not my boss, so get off my back!" We learn to *Deny*. "Of course I love you." Or, "I was in Milwaukee the day you said I did it." Or, "No, I don't want your job." We learn to *Defame*. "You're an idiot!" "You're another!" "It's all your fault." "You never *were* much." And finally, we learn to *Depart*. Split. Scram. Disappear, if only into the security of our heads and thoughts.

Even these layers of Onion Skin will go when we decide to quit using them. Each time I become aware that I am using one of them, I can quit! Losing them is small loss, since they

*I am indebted to Robert Tucker for this perfect analogy.

don't work most of the time and they aren't really "me" anyway. They're learned behaviors.

What are you liable to find underneath the Skins? A unique person. You! How will you look? How should I know? It's been years since that "you" has seen the light of day. The chances are that you'll like what you find. One of the nice aspects of the way I earn my living is that I get to watch people peel away dried out old Onion Skins and discover to their delight that there is One Neat Person underneath—warm, tender, loving, clever, imaginative and creative, excited, open and nurturing—all of the things, in fact, that folk had been saying he or she should have been. That person was there all along!

What were you designed to be? I'm willing to share four ideas that occur to me:

We are designed to be creatures *who enjoy being alive.* Somebody—I lost the name somehow—wrote a fine statement: "On judgment day, we will each have to give account for all the things we refused to enjoy." In *Franny and Zooey,* J. D. Salinger claims that "religion is what God sics on people who have the gall to accuse him of having created an ugly world." We are surrounded by beauty, and I won't believe it was put here just to tempt us. When I am feeling put together and not busy trying to "make something out of myself," I usually have the inclination to enjoy myself, even while working. Why not?

We are designed to be *creatures who experience.* Ever watch a cat? My friend Bandit is watching me type right now. He's fascinated. Every time the carriage returns, he jumps. He is intrigued with what's happening. (He must have decided he'd experienced enough of that; now he's on the table experiencing how his fur tastes.) One of life's great intimacies is simply being "with" what's going on around us.

I am more than somewhat grateful for the person(s) who

taught me that life is a smorgasbord. There is so much to do, to experience. One of my cardinal rules of life has been to not miss a new experience. I've set some boundaries. There are some things I have never done, nor will I ever do them. But within my boundaries, I go full steam ahead. I've earned money in twenty or thirty kinds of work, from taxi driver to milkman, from millwright to bus driver, from pastor to psychotherapist. These weren't "accomplishments," they were *experiences*. They were new ways of getting in touch with my world.

I've experienced my world in other ways. I've had half a dozen hobbies, studied nine languages, and traveled every chance I've had. My car radio's push-buttons are set for five different types of music programming.

For the same reason I've even eaten some of every foodstuff that came my way, from cold sliced lamb eyeballs to fried brain sandwiches, from sweet-and-sour tongue to pickled eel. (Broccoli is still at the bottom of my list.) Life is one incredible adventure after another, and I'm the only one who can keep it from being so.

This leads me to the third thing I think we were designed to be: *creatures who learn and grow*. There is no way you can experience life without learning. When will we quit trying to cram knowledge into people as if learning were something that required force? You can't help learning when the learning climate is right. There is usually no way you can learn something without growing. I believe we have an innate propensity for healthy growth. The question is never "How can I make that happen?" but "How am I keeping myself from growing?" or "What (like illness or booze or deprivation) is keeping me from growing?"

What are we supposed to grow into? Who knows? That's the mystery of life. *We haven't "happened" yet.* I can tell you what other folk have grown into, but only when their lives were finished. Paul wrote that "it is not yet apparent what we shall become." I really like that line. If I knew what I was going to end up looking like, life might be a tad more secure but it surely would be "one long dental appointment, interrupted occasionally by something exciting, like waiting or falling asleep." *

Finally, I think we were designed to be *creatures who produce,* but not necessarily producing what we usually refer to these days. By production I mean the effect we have on our environment. As we experience our world, we interact with it in a way that results in something being produced. Sometimes we produce *things.* Marie Curie took some stuff—pitchblende—and produced radium. We make "things" with our minds and our muscles—meat loaves or statues, poems or purses, paintings or barns. I have never met a person who didn't want to produce something, some thought, some feeling. We get into trouble when we tell folk, whom we're not paying, how much to produce (of what kind) and on what sort of schedule. Some of my most productive writing times occur when I'm still cranking up. From the outside I don't imagine it looks like much—staring, reading, wandering about, doodling on scratch paper. Without that pregnant "nothing period," nothing would ever come out.

We also produce when we interact with other people. The woman who heard that dog of a sermon received a lot, yet I didn't even know she was there. Many people have had fantastic effects on my life just by being in my life. In college, a little Greek woman named Kay Flores literally turned my life around one day by giving me a note. I still carry that piece of torn-out notebook paper with me.

Though I barely knew her, she lovingly gave me some information about myself that I wasn't seeing. She suggested a new

*Murray Burns in Herb Gardner's *A Thousand Clowns*

way to behave. All in about five sentences. I scarcely saw her after that short encounter. I tried to write her twenty years later to say thank you but she seems to have disappeared. That "little happenstance" was one of the most important things in my life. I'll bet she has no idea of her impact. Don't tell me that woman isn't productive. As far as I'm concerned, she has produced enough to justify a hundred years of living with one short act.

So, when we are experiencing, learning and growing, enjoying and producing, we are *perfect*. We are doing what we were designed to do. We will each do these things differently

s being hauled in to perform that ceremony, she
, that's too much trouble; we're going to do it

preacher weren't the deliverer of God's truth, nor
changed wafers and Welch's into the Holy Pres-
e only one who could keep babies out of Limbo;
eren't any longer the person (parson) who was
everyone else, then what in Heaven or Hell was
ll problem. Men of the cloth began bailing out of
like the 101st Airborne did from their planes.
stayed kept wandering around trying to be some-
cant, unless they never had any pretensions to
lt was those who had a "role" who got confused
e disappeared.
parents. In a recent survey advertised by a news-
ologist, 70 percent of the parents surveyed said if
do it over again, they wouldn't be parents. We've
rom "cheaper by the dozen" to "more than two is
Childless couples are clearly increasing. "Why
e kids just so I can spend twenty-five years being
d outnumbered?"
g a business person isn't easy these days. The
Straw Boss are numbered. Participatory democ-
where, including the United States Navy. Only a
ger treats subordinates like subordinates.
ot is that more and more people are retreating
of social concern and social responsibility. The
f being responsible to and for other people is in
we were saying "to hell with it; I'm going to spend
ling with something I can get a handle on—ME!
figure out what's going on with me, take care of
myself in shape and let everybody else do the

tely, since we keep bumping into each other

4

Stand Still So I Can Comb Your Hair

I AM MY BROTHER'S KEEPER

I have days when I feel like the manager of an asylum when all the inmates are loose! I have a general idea of what is supposed to happen, but my plan doesn't fit anything going on around me. I'm supposed to do something, but my ducks just won't stand still long enough for me to get them lined up. (I learned from my mother, Big Edna, that "lining up your ducks" is Pretty Important.)

Somebody once wrote that the greatest curse a person can suffer is to live in "great times," and we are living in some great times! The curse is that we are *confused!* When life was simpler, as before World War II, a guy at least knew a thing or two *for sure.* God came calling on Sundays regardless of what the people did (if you weren't married you probably were going to hell no matter how good you were) and everyone knew the difference between Good Guys and Bad Guys. Above all, you knew to whom and for what you were responsible.

The whole issue of responsibility was fairly clear. Society had its "act together," and right or wrong the word was out. "Here's the person you're responsible for." Fathers and mothers knew what they were supposed to do. They might decide *not* to do it, but they knew they *should*. If they didn't, the telephones got busy and folk talked about how the Fang-schleisters were messing up. Not much argument.

Parents were supposed to make all the important decisions for their kids, provide all the necessities of life, arrange their social activities, and make damnsure that the kids Shaped Up. They had a lot of good sayings to guide them, such as "Children should be seen and not heard." They knew that people were "children" until they got to vote at age twenty-one. It wasn't always easy to make everything happen the way it was supposed to, but the guidelines were clear. If you produced a child, intentionally or from "messing around," you were totally responsible for him or her for twenty-one long years whether you liked it or not. Responsibility meant developing the values of the child, doing its thinking, and making it all happen. Parents worried a lot, but they weren't confused.

How about preachers? They had it nailed down. Their job was to be the God-selected people who were responsible for *everybody,* at least within geographical or organizational lines. If someone spent too much time sitting around drawing sexy pictures in his head (I say "his" because it was also clear in those days that women never *did* that kind of thing) then the preacher was supposed to do something about it, if only pray. But he *was* responsible for their "souls" and for what folk felt and thought and did, which pretty well covered the waterfront.

He was the guy who wore the special clothes and did all the very special acts, such as baptizing babies and passing out the wafers and wine during communion. He was the only guy in town who could talk for twenty-five minutes without getting any back talk. He had the last word on everything, and if he didn't, he was supposed to make it up. People got upset if he didn't.

He was supposed to pass
time I tried to leave a hospital
Gramma Josie had spent th
about some international car
ceries of America. (She was i
all bad!) After we wore out th
started to leave. "Aincha
barked, bowing her head an
four-year-old fashion. I did. I
ceries. Preachers were suppo

With the Quadruple Ren
clouding of roles. It didn't all
Slowly our roles began to mo
from some old ones. I recall
clergy endured. First came
longer did Laymen's Sunda
graciously relinquished our p
a brave imitation of what "rea
ous that *anyone* can preach
Reverner of having the who
ever thought he did, but at le
its mouth shut if it disagree
Word.

Justices of the peace had
"perverts," but everyone kne
ried in the eyes of God. No
Church weddings are nicer,
they have to take a drink to g
no one suggests anymore tha
in sin.

Changes also happened wi
wide women's retreat, a good
with the Blessed Sacrament.

ner who w
replied, "O
ourselves."

Well, if a
the one wh
ence, nor th
and if he
smarter tha
he? No sm
their pulpit
Those who
thing signifi
begin with.
when the ro

Same wi
paper psyc
they had to
quickly slid
mindless."
should I ha
confused a

Even be
days of the
racy is ever
dumb man
The ups
from areas
whole idea
flux. It's as
my time de
I'm going t
myself, ge
same."

Unfortur

(which isn't hard, given that there are so many of us around) we can't quite escape the problem of how we fit together. What if you already have some children? Or a wife or husband? Or a mother? How do you deal with the pesky brother who always gets his feelings hurt when you take a nap instead of looking at his new mulch pile? Where do you draw the line between your needs and hers when she wants you to quit playing golf and start going to more PTA bake-offs?

However far we've moved in the past two decades, we haven't shaken the notion that somehow we *are* responsible to and for others. We're not clear how we can be both responsible and autonomous; but we *have* been taught early that we are, in fact, responsible!

> *Mom:* Shame on you for hitting Billy!
> *Bob:* But, mom! He started the fight.
> *Mom:* Yes, but you're older.
>
> *Mom:* Go to sleep; I'm your mother and I know you're tired.
>
> *Dad:* I know what's good for you; I'm your father.
>
> *Mom:* Bobby, now that daddy's gone, you're the man of the family.
> *Bob:* But, mom! I'm only eight!

Little by little, we learn that there are all kinds of relationships, and there are distinct "pecking orders" involved. Watching others, it seems that the world is composed of Keepers and Keepees. There are some people who are supposed to keep me, and those who are kept by me. Even "religion" seems to support that. Remember how Cain, after knocking off his brother Abel, tried to weasel out of what he did? When God asked him where Abel was, Cain answered in a small-alecky way, "Well, how should I know? Am I my brother's keeper?" Are you aware that Cain, the farmer, killed Abel, the hunter, because Abel's offering of meat had pleased God (society?) and his own offering of grain had been rejected by this whimsical god? Our primitive fathers who told this story were hunters who had little use for the squatting farmer.

Sure, we're our brother's keeper! Everyone knows that. We're our sister's keeper too! Husbands are expected to be responsible for their wives. "You'd think he'd control his wife better than that!" A husband is legally responsible for all his wife's debts unless he takes legal action to head off that responsibility. He's also morally responsible for the family's welfare, *even if he's dead.* Lots of insurance or savings needed for that.

Mothers are held responsible for what their children do. "How can you let him ruin his life by being an artist?" "See how your kids dress? You must be a rotten mother!" "A mother should give her all for the children. After all, you brought them into the world." "You should teach him to like broccoli; all my children do."

It's everywhere, it's everywhere! "Why don't you tell him for his own good? (After all, you are responsible for everyone knowing everything.)" Or how about the poor navy captain? However glorious and plush his life, he pays one humongous price for it. He is literally responsible for everyone's actions aboard, *even while he's sleeping!* If his helmsman goes berserk and rams the cruiser on a reef, guess who's to blame? Wow!

The Vice-President-for-Deportment says to a department manager, "Herman, one of your boys really got bent out of shape at the party last night. That's a bad reflection on you, boy!" No small wonder we spend so much of our time acting like CIA agents—doing espionage and sabotage on those around us and then using the SS technique. We can either sneak or storm in an effort to make "the world we're responsible for" come out right.

By the time we were eighteen months old we were already veterans of "separation anxiety," as the psychologists term it. We experienced mom leaving the room, and we didn't even know how that occurred! Now the problem was how to get her back with the milk. We figured out that we were supposed to act in very precise ways to get her to come back and take care of us. Over and over we experienced "the fact" that to get our needs met we had to persuade people to move into the right place or position. Those early years, when our very survival depended on other people, we were taught lessons that are hard to unlearn.

Most relationships of "concern" are ultimately those of *control*. Two people battle, trying to get each other in the "right" place so the rest of their world will fit together. Since I am so obviously responsible for you in so many ways, goes the rationale, and since society (and apparently even my God) expects me to be your keeper, and since I know from early experiences that getting my needs met is dependent on you being in the right place, I obviously must figure out some way of controlling what you do. That is the tough one!

Each of us gets that settled, as Transactional Analysis has shown so clearly, by employing sneaky maneuvers—transactions that appear to go in one direction but really go in another. *

Let me show you how we learn that. You're six and playing with your older brother in the sandpile. Mom has given you each a couple of cookies. Big Bubba has decided he's hungrier than you and solves his problem by swiping your second

---

*For more information on these games we play, see my book, *No Grown-Ups in Heaven*, Chapter 11.

cookie. What can you do? You've got three choices. You could pretend you're not hungry and forget the whole thing, but you *are* hungry and feeling ripped-off, so that strikes you as a poor choice. You can reach over, punch his face out and take your cookie back. Or you can stand in the middle of the sandpile and cry until someone comes and rescues you. Either Bubba will get tired of the noise and go get you a cookie, or mom will come out to investigate. If she's any kind of Good American Mom, *she* will punch Bubba for ripping you off! Thirdly, you can be "helpful" by going back into the kitchen, explaining the situation to mom, and getting some more cookies for yourself. While you are there, you can drop some Helpful Hints about Bubba's Moral Fiber, which seems to be slipping; and say that if *somebody* doesn't punch him he will probably end up like Al Capone. (You'd just be telling mom that for Bubba's own good, right?)

As years go by, we learn to sophisticate these methods, and learn which method to use in each situation. We learn that some are more effective than others, although we invariably end up being victimized to some degree or other when using them. If mom explains that she will not allow any more cookies before supper, no matter *what* happened, we feel victimized. The best we can hope for now is the slim pleasure of watching Bubba get what's coming to him, as the expression goes.

We're all accustomed to feeling like victims. Figuring it's inevitable, we learn to settle for reducing the *amount* of victimization. We can do that by using one of our three methods. The Out-Front-Victim knows how to pout and look Put-Upon, hoping that someone will feel bad and take care of him. (If you doubt the effectiveness of this, watch a two-year-old when someone says no to him. Chin drooping, lower lip pushed out, eyes wet, a hangdog expression—all are guaranteed to make *someone* say, "For heaven's sakes, Henry! How can you do that to one of these little ones? Give him the cookie, you child beater!")

Playing the victim is tough work and therefore used consistently *only* by the real pros. The rest of us minimize our victimization with our more typical Sneak and Storm techniques. The Sneaker begins his attack by out-helping everyone. He does piles and gobs of good things for others. Later on, The Sneaker gets to say, "After all I've done for you, Schnook, I expect you to. . . ." The secret, of course, lies in keeping folk in debt.

Some people find Being Helpful a great big pain. They prefer the Storm method. If you want people to do something, you just hit them first! The people who hang around the Toddle Inn Bar 'n' Grill do it with their fists. The rest of us do it with our mouths. ZAP! The theory is that people Shape Up when beat around the head and shoulders long enough. So rub their noses in it. Works with dogs, doesn't it? "What's wrong with you is. . . ." "There, you've gone and done it again!" "You've always. . . ." "You never. . . ." "Why don't you ever. . . ."

Is that the way life is? There is a lot of Helping and Zapping and Whining going on. Guess it must always be that way, and there isn't much we can do about it. Want a surprise? *I'm not your keeper! Never was and never will be!* You're not anybody's keeper, and no one is your keeper. There are four exceptions: Children under six obviously have to have keepers. Animals usually have keepers, especially if the animals are in a zoo. Some of the people in locked psychiatric wards need keepers. Convicts at the "Barbed Wire Motel" have keepers, but that's almost the entire list. Nobody else has keepers. We just think we do.

Well, what about God and Cain and all that? Didn't God himself say that Cain was his brother's keeper? Didn't He? As a matter of fact, the answer is *no*. God didn't say that, even in the story. Cain, having "slew his brother in the head," thought he saw a way out of the mounting confrontation with God. By pointing out that he wasn't being *paid* to keep track of his brother's whereabouts, he hoped God might back down.

Cain's question, "Am I my brother's keeper?" was really a statement. Fritz Perls said that a question is a statement with a hook on the end of it. If someone makes a statement with a question, answering it will only get you deeper into the quicksand! God didn't bite. Instead of getting sidetracked into some discussion about who keeps whom, he simply demanded that Cain be responsible for Cain. *"What have you done?"* he insisted. "Your brother's blood is crying to me from the ground." Cain was *not* his brother's keeper; but he surely was his brother's *brother.* He *was* responsible for what he himself had done.

That makes a difference in the whole responsibility issue. Trying to be responsible for other persons who are over ten years of age is untenable, both psychologically and theologically, unless you can lock them up somewhere. The law requires responsibility in certain relationships. Sometimes the law burdens people in a crazy way. For a parent to be held responsible for anything a fifteen-year-old does outside the home is an insane way of regulating things. The *kid* is responsible; let him be held so.

Again, we frequently assume responsibility for certain other people, or for tasks we have elected to fulfill. We usually put more into such a relationship, but the fact that we have decided to care for others does not give us, automatically, the right to stomp around in their lives.

If we decide to be responsible for another's life and act on that decision, we are interfering with that person's right to live her own life, regardless of our intentions. Telling ourselves that "God sent me here to keep you" doesn't change that fact. The old cliché that "God couldn't be everywhere so he invented mothers" puts a yukky load on mothers and chains on the kids.

I know a lady who's about to become an octogenarian. That's a lot of time-in-grade! At eighty, she's bright-eyed and bushy-tailed. Now a widow, she's doing a lot of things she's always wanted to do and she's quite a sight to behold. She chose to remain in the old family homestead during the past decade when the neighborhood changed from a sedate white neighborhood to a sedate black neighborhood.

She adapted to this situation the way she adapted to most. She decided to "keep on truckin'." She's made friends with the new people, knows all the kids, calls neighbors on the phone, passes out candy—all the usual neighborly things. The result is that she's happy in her neighborhood despite the change in color.

Not so, some of her relatives! They aren't pleased and are worried about her safety. They keep urging her to go an old folks' home where she will "be safe." This particular lady needs an old folks' home like she needs a book on childbirth. She could be happy in one *if* she were the manager, or the cook. She says, "Why would I want to go live with all those old fogies?" Why indeed?

My hunch is that these well-meaning people don't like *visiting* her where she is, or they don't like worrying, which they apparently insist on doing. If she moves, *they'll* feel better.

A father once asked me what to do about his son. The son had just bought a $900 stereo and the father was truly disturbed by this. Did the father think the stereo would blow up and kill his son and daughter-in-law? No, he was afraid "the kid" was still using bad judgment. (The "kid" was twenty-eight years old!) So long as he insisted on feeling responsible for a twenty-eight-year-old, both of them were going to be hassling one another and feeling bad.

Sometimes "being responsible for another" gets bloody. Remember the major in Vietnam who destroyed an entire village full of people in order to "save them from the enemy"?

Remember when, eager for someone to be responsible for them, the people turned themselves over to others who promised to deliver "law and order"—people named Nixon, Agnew, Mitchell?

Sometimes it isn't only the Kept who are victimized by the idea that we're responsible for everyone around us. Sometimes the *keeper* is in the cage. I know a number of people who are literally "wasted" by always saying yes when invited to take on the responsibilities of caring for someone else. They're suckers for anyone with a need or a demand or even a gentle request. If the flag goes up, they gotta salute it.

Being "responsible for others" always leads to Look-What-I-Did-For-Him, no matter how modest we are. After awhile, *that* turns into How-Could-She-Do-That-To-Me-After-What-I-Did-For-Her. Sometimes we even say that out loud!

OK, but what are we supposed to do about those other people?

Unfortunately, the two ways people relate to each other these days both seem rotten. One is to be responsible for others and expect them to return the favor. If that fails, we can always let the other guy have it with Both Barrels. (Sometimes we persecute people very gently by putting silencers on Both Barrels. They drop with a surprised look on their faces since they didn't hear the gun go off!) I don't think there's much virtue in that.

The other way of relating is getting more popular each day, but I think it is equally pitiful. Having learned that I am really only responsible for *me,* and you are only responsible for *you,* it's fairly easy to say, "Well, I'm just going to do whatever turns me on. If you don't like it, that's your problem." While it is technically true that we're only responsible for ourselves, and assuming the speaker isn't reading his magazine at the top of his voice in your ear or lying spread out across the dining room table while you're trying to eat, such an attitude can lead to some pretty cold-blooded operations. When Elmer says to Emma, "Go see your shrink if you don't like my playing bagpipes while you read," he can *expect* some yelling. Old Elmer doesn't sound like much fun to be around, and he isn't acting very interested in Emma *for sure.*

There's a third choice! We don't have to choose between being responsible and being indifferent, cold-blooded slobs. We can be *responsive.* Here are a couple of ways being responsive might look. Let's say Agnes has just complained about her husband's reading. "A fine man you are, sitting there reading all the time!" Her husband, Sylvester, is a liberated man, meaning he's aware he doesn't read all the time, knows that reading silently is not an irritating act, and understands that Emma wants something from him. Therefore, he is willing to be responsive to her.

Possibility A:

Syl: What are you wanting?

Agnes: Well, I sure would like to talk about our day.

Syl: Lemme finish this article, and I'll be happy to talk for an hour or so; and then I want to finish the magazine. OK?

Possibility B:

Syl: What are you wanting?

Agnes: I don't want anything. I just think it's wrong for a man to sit around reading all the time.

Syl: How do you see that being wrong?

Agnes: Well, it's like you're going off all by yourself where no one can get to you.

Syl: So when I read, you get to feeling abandoned?

> *Agnes:* Yeah! My dad used to read whenever he wanted to get away from us kids. I always felt like I was invisible.
>
> *Syl:* Well, you're sure not invisible to me. Let's move our chairs closer together while I read and you knit. And I'll share interesting items. OK?

I'm aware that if Aggie-baby really wants to hit Syl a lick, *nothing* he says or does is going to work. You can usually translate "work" into "making the other guy act the way you want him to act." If Agnes refuses to budge from her attack, Syl will have to deal with getting hit. He could say, "Hey, I'm willing to talk with you and to stop reading for awhile. I am *not* willing to let you beat on me and I want you to stop it. If you won't, then what I'm going to do is. . . . Which do you want?" He's still being very responsive to Aggie and what's going on, while he takes care of himself.

The difference between "being responsible" and "being responsive" is considerable. Once you get the idea, it's fairly easy to tell the difference.

Take the example of the mom or dad who is still combing a ten-year-old kid's hair without asking if he *wants* it combed. Responsible parents will wage all out war over messed-up hair. Usually, the real reason for the war is based on something like this:

> *"Well, if he goes to school looking that way the teacher will think I'm a bad mother!"* (If the teacher thinks that, *she's* wrong; most teachers will think Johnny doesn't comb his hair.)

> *"Well, if I don't make him comb it, he'll have messed-up hair when he's thirty."* (Nonsense! The chances are nine

4

Stand Still So I Can Comb Your Hair

I AM MY BROTHER'S KEEPER

I have days when I feel like the manager of an asylum when all the inmates are loose! I have a general idea of what is supposed to happen, but my plan doesn't fit anything going on around me. I'm supposed to do something, but my ducks just won't stand still long enough for me to get them lined up. (I learned from my mother, Big Edna, that "lining up your ducks" is Pretty Important.)

Somebody once wrote that the greatest curse a person can suffer is to live in "great times," and we are living in some great times! The curse is that we are *confused!* When life was simpler, as before World War II, a guy at least knew a thing or two *for sure.* God came calling on Sundays regardless of what the people did (if you weren't married you probably were going to hell no matter how good you were) and everyone knew the difference between Good Guys and Bad Guys. Above all, you knew to whom and for what you were responsible.

The whole issue of responsibility was fairly clear. Society had its "act together," and right or wrong the word was out. "Here's the person you're responsible for." Fathers and mothers knew what they were supposed to do. They might decide *not* to do it, but they knew they *should*. If they didn't, the telephones got busy and folk talked about how the Fang-schleisters were messing up. Not much argument.

Parents were supposed to make all the important decisions for their kids, provide all the necessities of life, arrange their social activities, and make damnsure that the kids Shaped Up. They had a lot of good sayings to guide them, such as "Children should be seen and not heard." They knew that people were "children" until they got to vote at age twenty-one. It wasn't always *easy* to make everything happen the way it was supposed to, but the guidelines were clear. If you produced a child, intentionally or from "messing around," you were totally responsible for him or her for twenty-one long years whether you liked it or not. Responsibility meant developing the values of the child, doing its thinking, and making it all happen. Parents worried a lot, but they weren't confused.

How about preachers? They had it nailed down. Their job was to be the God-selected people who were responsible for *everybody*, at least within geographical or organizational lines. If someone spent too much time sitting around drawing sexy pictures in his head (I say "his" because it was also clear in those days that women never *did* that kind of thing) then the preacher was supposed to do something about it, if only pray. But he *was* responsible for their "souls" and for what folk felt and thought and did, which pretty well covered the water-front.

He was the guy who wore the special clothes and did all the very special acts, such as baptizing babies and passing out the wafers and wine during communion. He was the only guy in town who could talk for twenty-five minutes without getting any back talk. He had the last word on everything, and if he didn't, he was supposed to make it up. People got upset if he didn't.

He was supposed to pass out blessings. I remember the first time I tried to leave a hospital room without "having a prayer." Gramma Josie had spent the last twenty minutes telling me about some international cartel that was taking over the groceries of America. (She was in for a tune-up and not feeling at all bad!) After we wore out that subject and exchanged trivia, I started to leave. "Aincha gonna give me a prayer?" she barked, bowing her head and folding her hands in her best four-year-old fashion. I did. I remembered to include the groceries. Preachers were supposed to pray in hospitals.

With the Quadruple Renaissance came the fuzzing and clouding of roles. It didn't all happen on a Tuesday morning. Slowly our roles began to move into new areas and withdraw from some old ones. I recall vividly the identity crises that we clergy endured. First came the "ministry of the laity." No longer did Laymen's Sunday suffice. (That was the day we graciously relinquished our pulpits to someone who would do a brave imitation of what "real preachers" did.) Now, it is obvious that *anyone* can preach, and no one accuses the poor Reverner of having the whole truth! I don't suppose anyone ever thought he did, but at least society knew enough to keep its mouth shut if it disagreed with his version of the Holy Word.

Justices of the peace had always performed marriages for "perverts," but everyone knew these folk weren't really married in the eyes of God. Now, that distinction is dissolved. Church weddings are nicer, so most folk want one even if they have to take a drink to get through the strange ritual; but no one suggests anymore that the secularly married are living in sin.

Changes also happened with Holy Communion. At a state-wide women's retreat, a good weekend once was to conclude with the Blessed Sacrament. When I asked the program planner who was being hauled in to perform that ceremony, she replied, "Oh, that's too much trouble; we're going to do it ourselves."

Well, if a preacher weren't the deliverer of God's truth, nor the one who changed wafers and Welch's into the Holy Presence, nor the only one who could keep babies out of Limbo; and if he weren't any longer the person (parson) who was smarter than everyone else, then what in Heaven or Hell was he? No small problem. Men of the cloth began bailing out of their pulpits like the 101st Airborne did from their planes. Those who stayed kept wandering around trying to be something significant, unless they never had any pretensions to begin with. It was those who had a "role" who got confused when the role disappeared.

Same with parents. In a recent survey advertised by a newspaper psychologist, 70 percent of the parents surveyed said if they had to do it over again, they wouldn't be parents. We've quickly slid from "cheaper by the dozen" to "more than two is mindless." Childless couples are clearly increasing. "Why should I have kids just so I can spend twenty-five years being confused and outnumbered?"

Even being a business person isn't easy these days. The days of the Straw Boss are numbered. Participatory democracy is everywhere, including the United States Navy. Only a *dumb* manager treats subordinates like subordinates.

The upshot is that more and more people are retreating from areas of social concern and social responsibility. The whole idea of being responsible to and for other people is in flux. It's as if we were saying "to hell with it; I'm going to spend my time dealing with something I can get a handle on—ME! I'm going to figure out what's going on with me, take care of myself, get myself in shape and let everybody else do the same."

Unfortunately, since we keep bumping into each other

out of ten that the kid will be extremely careful of his hair shortly after he "discovers" girls.)

"My boss would fire me if I let my hair go that way." (The boy doesn't work for your boss. He's a schoolboy.)

"I feel bad when I see his hair look that way." (So how come a ten-year-old is supposed to be responsible for how mom decides to feel? She can quit looking if she wants.)

Responsive parents will treat their children as if the kids might just possibly be able to understand and reason.

> *Mom:* I really like how you look with your hair combed.
> *Jim:* Sometimes I comb it. Like for church.
> *Mom:* So how come you don't do that for school?
> *Jim:* Only the class sissy and the girls comb their hair, mom. We're too busy playing stickball to mess with that girl stuff.
> *Mom:* Yeah. I remember how the boys in my fifth grade class always messed up Percival's hair.
> *Jim:* Boy, things haven't changed much!

This mom knows that it's *his* hair and he can do with it what he wants, and probably will. She is willing to let Jim get picked on, or scolded by teachers, if he likes. And she wisely realizes he will comb it when it suits *his* purposes (not hers).

But what about the time it really *does* get in mom's way? Let's say he never washes his hair and the grease stains the pillowcases? She still has a couple of responsive choices beside complaining or scolding. For example, she can cover the pillowcases with plastic baggies and explain that they stay on until his hair is cleaner. Or she can decide simply that two pillowcases belong to Jim, however black they get. My hunch would be that one day he'll start feeling crabby about the feel or looks of his pillows and want to do something about that. If not, *no one* has a problem.

5

Doing Good and Feeling Bad

DO UNTO OTHERS AS YOU WOULD HAVE OTHERS DO UNTO YOU

If anything is sacred in life, it's the Golden Rule. It was taught by Confucius, Lao-tsu, Plato and the Old Testament; Jesus himself made it popular. A kid might forget most of the other things he was taught in Sunday school, but he will remember that we are supposed to do unto others as you would have others do unto you.

I've never heard anyone argue against it. Even mildly! It is the "headline" for most folk's ethical system. It gives us the main idea for dealing with each other. It's the problem solver that tells us what to buy another guy for his birthday or how to tell him his fly is open or what to do when he's tired or crabby.

Dad is enthusiastic about body building. He likes to think of himself as an athlete. He used to be the star halfback for the Doby High Raiders; now he plays shortstop for his company's softball team. More than anything, he likes people to tell him he plays well. His son's birthday is coming up, so it's Golden Rule time. "What would I like to get for my birthday if I were sixteen?" he wonders. There's no question about that! He trots over to the local sporting-goods store and buys a complete softball outfit—bat, ball, spiked shoes, hat, glove, and "unmentionables" to go with them. "Boy! He'll take one look at this stuff and know how much I love him. He's gonna be *so* excited!"

As the boy opens his gifts with glazed-over eyes, he wonders why his dad missed the rather obvious fact that he is skinny, unathletic and couldn't hit a bull in the rear end with a ball bat if he were standing on its tail. He had hoped for the latest Chicago recording. He mumbles a "thank you ver' much" and goes to don his headset and drown his sorrow with a cadenza or two. Dad is left feeling confused and unappreciated. "If I was him, I'd be ecstatic! The kid must not like me. Where'd I go wrong?"

I once knew a guy in Okinawa. Never in my life did I want to hit a man so badly. He did what he liked to call "lay missionary work," because he wanted the Orientals to "know Jesus." He carried a box of sugar cubes in his coat pocket. Since he really liked sugar, he figured everyone else did. Whenever he got within striking distance of some gentle Ryukuan, he would cram a sugar cube into the poor guy's mouth and intone his ritual. "Jesus loves you." The sugar cubes were a vital part of his "ministry."

Oriental culture forbids insulting another person, so to spit out the sugar would be an insufferable insult. Rather than do that, those given the cubes would smile (with unsmiling eyes) and swallow. The "missionary" complained that his work for Jesus wasn't having much success. No one asked to join his church. I suppose it never occurred to him that he was perpetrating a form of rape on the other person. He may have comforted himself with the knowledge that he was following the Golden Rule.

There has to be a special place in Hell for people like him! I still wonder how many diabetics he threw into a coma or how many Orientals still flee Americans in general to protect themselves from the Big Sugar Cube.

These examples are extreme and "dumb." But why *doesn't* the Golden Rule work sometimes? Sometimes it works well.

"Doing to others" first requires that we figure out the other person. What's she want? What will be listened to? How much will be put up with? What will persuade him to do what I want?

If we usually take responsibility for knowing what others want, we can still only *guess*. We must get in the person's head and figure out what we'd do if we were in her place. "If I were you I would. . . ." Wrong! *If you were I, you would do exactly what I do!* (Greer's Fourth Law of Existence). Period. Guessing what people want, or need, or will do, works about 60 percent of the time at best; 40 percent of the time we fall on our faces trying to "figure out" the other guy.

Projecting is the act of pretending we're in someone else's head and in touch with what he thinks or feels. "He's feeling sorry for me." "She thinks she's so tough." "He wants me to hug him." This can cause trouble unless we have long and accurate experience. Even with our mates our experiences may not have made us all that accurate. We can decide what we would be thinking or feeling if we were acting in a particular way. But then we must *project* our thoughts and feelings to the other guy, and risk a 40 percent chance of being off target. I wouldn't cross the street against those odds, and neither am I willing to cross life's street with the odds stacked against me. What we need to know in these situations is not what *we* would do—we already know that. We need to know what *they* would do.

I like the story about the man who ate peanut butter and jelly sandwiches out of his lunchbox for thirty years. He hated peanut butter and jelly sandwiches, but he figured that was what his wife wanted him to eat. She made them every day and he knew *he* wouldn't do that unless he really wanted the other person to eat them! So he consumed them with humility and gratitude for her love but without much enthusiasm. For her part, she *hated* making the damned things! Gooey! But he ate them so vigorously and so constantly that he must want them. *She* wouldn't eat anything day after day unless she was crazy about it! She kept making them and he kept eating them. Neither bothered to check with the other. Dumb! And it happens a lot.

The Big Motto that we should "do unto others as we would have others do unto us" is a part of our group Conceptual Grid. *How* to "do unto others" is usually explained by our own Conceptual Grid. Our own value decisions define both how we should act and what the other person ought to want. A ten-year-old, for example, is reading a comic book on the couch. She is in her normal posture—sprawled and gangling, half upside down—like a sideshow contortionist. Dad's belief-system reports that he would be uncomfortable in such a position. "No one is comfortable upside down," so *she* can't be comfortable. He likes to lie straight, with a pillow under his head and maybe an afghan over him. So he "does unto her!" Wop, pull, crank, plop. Now he's helped the kid be "comfortable." So why is she storming out of the house muttering nonsense about how nobody around the house cares about anyone else? Didn't she just get "done unto"? Maybe she's flunking puberty. Maybe he ought to take her to see a shrink!

People can get surly even when nurture is meant to be helpful, and will, if the nurture annoys them. The Golden Rule does *not* give us permission to be "gracious Nazis" who get to ram our ideas of the way life ought to be lived into other folk under the banner of "kindness." When we try we usually get into trouble. "She should like the sexy underwear I bought her." "Why won't he read the *Houston Business Journal* I bought him; it would help him so much." "You'd be able to read better if the light were brighter." "You really look nice in the clothes I bought you, dear."

Our nurturing of other people is not always altruistic. In fact, it is *never* without some degree of self-interest. If I decide to send a hundred dollars to the Society for Spastic Needle Threaders, I am somehow fulfilling a need that I have, in addition to caring for the SSNT. All behavior meets a need! I do what I do because it somehow helps me get through the day. Or the year. Finding out how I take care of my own needs is not always easy and takes a lot of awareness.

Velma spends days drawing intricate and lacy greeting cards to give her friend, Larry Don, on holidays. They are exquisite. He is six feet tall and "all man." He opens them, grunts and fastens them to his closet door with thumb tacks— right through the middle—and seldom looks at them again. "How can he *do* that?" wails Velma. "I'd give anything to get something that beautiful!"

The point is, sometimes we "do unto others" as a way of getting them to act or feel the way we want them to. This happens in subtle ways and is frequently below our awareness. The dad who rearranged his daughter's reading posture probably was consciously thinking only of her; he might be surprised to realize that he also very much wanted her to see him as a caring, nurturing father and *to smile at him.*

Scene: A husband drags himself home from work, tired yet overstimulated. The world has rattled his cage one too many times. His nerve ends feel like dandelions-gone-to-seed look. Sprung! Right now he wants a tomb more than anything else. He wants to pretend he's died and gone to Heaven. He wants what is called peace and quiet. He walks into the house of an equally frantic woman, but his wife is frantic for a different reason. She has spent her entire day with a one-year-old and a two-year-old and has had a total of thirty-six minutes of "conversation" with them. After eight of them, she was already sick of pretending that their "nahney-noonies" were important human dialogue. Now she is *wild* for adult human contact. She wants a real live grown-up human being who talks in whole words and sentences. She wants to carry only half the responsibility for a conversation.

Both mates have serious needs and they intend to have them met. She is so happy to see another mortal, let alone her husband, that she lands on him the way the morning newspaper hits the front porch. Her mouth imitates a teletype machine. How does he solve his problem? He pretends he can't understand English and is a deaf-mute to boot. "Mrmmmph. . . . Nnnnnnnnn . . . Ummmmmmmmm . . . Ehhhhhhh." She wants conversation, so she talks a lot. He wants silence, so he returns deathly silence.

Scene: (Later that night, in bed) Things have settled down. It's Kiddie Time for the big people. The little ones finally have been nailed into bed. Now it's time for a little "Hey, we're alone!" activity. They crawl into their bed without their "jammies," a signal that they're both ready to Not Sleep. As they hug each other, loving hands move across each other's skin. But how differently! She likes to be tickled lightly—those feathery, tingly, light-touched strokes that give her goose bumps. He likes heavy rubbing—long, smooth, hard pressures that relax his muscles and make him feel wanted and safe.

So as they hug, she tickles his back and neck. He rubs her like a men's club masseur. After five minutes of this, both are about to come unstapled. He is thinking, "My God, this woman is over-active. Maybe her motor's stuck! I was almost calmed down, but now I'm about to crawl out of my skin. I'll give her three more minutes to quit and if she doesn't, I'm gonna fix myself a martini!"

She is thinking, "Can't he tell I'm just a *little* girl? He's rubbing the skin right off my bones. I'll have to lay in Jergen's lotion for a month to get well again. Maybe he fell asleep and is having a dream about erasing the blackboard. If he keeps it up, I'm going to hear the baby crying!"

Five minutes later, he's in the kitchen adding vermouth to

some gin, wondering if he is on the road to becoming an "alkie." She is diapering a baby who wonders why he was awakened from a sound sleep. "Why doesn't my mommie work *days* like all the others?"

A love relationship is suffering a four-week setback resulting from a ten-minute act of affection. What went wrong? Ironically, both people were unwittingly following the Golden Rule while failing to give to, or get from, the other person information about what they indeed wanted. Instead each was simply doing to the other what each wanted done.

When we use the Golden Rule, either consciously or unconsciously, and it doesn't work, we end up feeling either impotent or unappreciated. This magnificent, age-old slogan *can* be misunderstood, reduced to a formula, or used in an inappropriate situation.

If you are going to use the Golden Rule, it may be useful to see it as a guideline rather than a formula. *Guidelines don't dictate behavior; they guide it!* "Do unto others as you would have others do unto you" invites us to consider other people's feelings and thoughts; it leads us to cooperation instead of competition. It can give us a more positive view and help us work together by being considerate of others. It suggests that we apply the same rules to others that *we* choose to live by.

Following the principle of the Golden Rule, then, we can find new ways to relate to other people. We can decide to give others the same freedom we expect and respect their opinions as we want ours respected.

The original Golden Rule, found in the Old Testament, was put negatively. "Don't do to others what you wouldn't want done to you." I prefer that. If I don't like to be scolded, I won't scold others. If I don't like "dirty tricks" played on me, I won't play them on you. If I don't like being "one-down," I won't invite others to feel one-down. Following the negative rule, I'm in no danger of forcing something on you that you don't want.

I've found that the Golden Rule is more consistently helpful when I think of it in still another way: Do unto others as *they* would have you do unto them. To do that successfully you gotta ask what they want!

Many times our experience and previous questioning tells us that we *are* doing what they want, but it doesn't hurt to check from time to time. "Do you still like peanut butter?" the wife in the story could have asked. Or just because someone wanted the thermostat at 80° yesterday doesn't mean she is feeling cold today. Staying current keeps us out of trouble.

I can't emphasize enough the usefulness of *checking*. More troublesome situations are caused by a lack of current, accurate information (or our refusal to *use* that information) than any other single thing. We plunge headlong into situations without knowing what we need to know, and then are awestruck when the axe falls on us. We can then only mumble, "Well, I thought. . . ."

Assuming no crisis is in progress, there is nothing wrong with deciding not to act until we are sure of our ground. In my "young lieutenant" days, I didn't want to appear ignorant (when I was). Frequently, upon hearing orders I didn't thoroughly understand, I would salute smartly and wander off in confusion. I made tough work for myself by trying to guess what in the world my C.O. had in mind. On occasion I guessed right, but usually I sweated a lot while goofing-up the project.

Ever make plans for the evening during breakfast? By dinner, though, you're feeling tired and cranky. Without checking, you go ahead with your plans, because *you* wouldn't want someone to back out at the last minute. Then, after a *terrible* evening, you discover your friend was tired, cranky, and following the same Golden Rule. You both could have checked with each other to see how you felt. It doesn't hurt to let others know where we stand. "Hey, we've been going bowling on Thursday nights for three hundred years, and I think I'm getting tired of it. Want to quit going?" Sometimes we find out the other guy is tired of it, too. If not, we can always go ahead and do what we planned.

6

You Should Have Thought of That First

YOU'VE MADE YOUR BED; NOW LIE IN IT

Sammy Fangschleister has completed four years of college and three of graduate school. With his Ph.D. nailed to the office wall, he has steadily and surely climbed the ladder of middle-management. He is on his way to becoming success-, ful, a quaint and popular way of saying "already successful but not yet satisfied." There is only one small hitch. He hates his job! He hates his vocation in general and the kinds of things he spends all day doing in particular. He doesn't like the kind of people he works with or the rules they go by.

Every day as he fights the freeway to and from the suburbs, he plays with the idea of doing something different. But what in the world would he do? All he knows is the engineering involved in building offshore oil rigs. He simply has too much invested to throw it all away now! He spent thirty thousand dollars and seven years of his life just learning all those numbers and formulas. He has worked six years to get ahead of all those other climbers who work for the Water-Cooled Slide Rule Engineering Corporation, Inc. Some of the top troops at WCSREC are beginning to call him by his first name.

Each time he considers changing vocation, he remembers

that old saying, You've made your bed; now lie in it! He *has* indeed made his bed. Carefully, and thoughtfully, and deliberately. It isn't as if he had gone into it lightly. But, damn-it-all! He's thirty-one years old and he *hates* numbers, formulas, file cabinets, drawings, and the rat race of endless meetings. He's changed a lot since he made his decision, but it's too late now. Well, what the heck? He can retire in thirty-four years.

"You've made your bed!" Wonder where that saying came from? From the Bible, or Shakespeare? Sounds more like something Big Bertha, my German grossmütter, made up. It's a very "common sense" understanding that pervades many of our lives. Given a decision, A, then it seems B, C, and D must follow relentlessly, unless something powerful intervenes mercifully and breaks the chain.

Leaving the air force after ten years was a really tough decision for me. I was a career officer and had planned to stay in for at least the full twenty years. I had been promoted to major, received a commendation medal, and my next assignment was to spend a year at the Air Command and Staff College. This pattern indicated that unless I really goofed-up, I had a good crack at the top. I really liked the military. Some general officers were following my career with interest. I loved the baubles and bangles, the way you could read a man's history on his sleeve and chest. I even liked saluting!

I wasn't so crazy about the killing my organization was involved in (in Southeast Asia) and the Peace is Our Profession motto was wearing pretty thin in my head. The real problem was that halfway through my career, most of my illusionary bubbles about the military chaplaincy had burst. I won't tell you the details, but it was clear to me that spending ten more years as a filing cabinet inspector and regulation quoter was *out!*

I entered a twelve-month period of real internal struggle. I knew I wanted out, but the thought of giving up goodies like uniforms and officers' clubs and world travel was painful. The *real obstacle* that hindered me was my understanding that I had made my bed and now I was trying to "weasel out of it." To leave the air force meant throwing it all away—wasting ten years of active duty. I suspected that I might not be throwing anything away, so I did resign. Ten years later, I'm aware that the only things I have missed out on were the pension that would start about now, and riding in staff cars.

"Making your bed" can refer to that suit of clothes you bought on impulse and now can't stand, so you decide either to wear it until it falls apart or hang it way back in the closet where you have some hope of forgetting it. (To give it to the Salvation Army would be "weaseling"!)

Or you try out that new recipe for ratatouille (the picture in the cookbook looked so fine!) and it horrifies your taste buds. But you gotta eat it! And what's more, you have to put the left-overs in the freezer! You made your bed, baby! So gird your loins for two more distasteful meals (unless you can foist off the leftovers on the new French lady who moved next door). This is not only a case of bed-making; it also has to do with "Waste not, want not." 'Member? Don't ever throw anything away.

Most folk apply the same rules to their life-styles. "I'm the kind of person who. . . ." is how they describe their way of living. ". . . who only likes to wear sedate (or wild) clothes." ". . . who eats on the run." ". . . who isn't handy with tools." This is who I am and there's no changing. "I decided to be a family man so there's no changing until there are 2.7 kids in the house!" (All of us has a number in our head that defines the correct number of children!)

This idea that once we choose our rut we must stay in it all the way is a deadly one. Ever get one of those invitations to visit a new country club housing development? No strings attached. They'll give you gas money for driving up there, free

meals, free lodging, and let you enjoy their tennis courts and swimming areas. All you have to commit yourself to is a thirty-minute tour and a short sales pitch. You are free to say no; there will be no bad feelings. How can they afford to do that? Easy! They've figured out the odds to the fifth decimal place. 7.47548 percent of the visitors will buy because they like what they see. Another 28.39748 percent will start to give in before they leave! "He's been so good to me! I *owe* him something! So what if I don't *want* the property. I shoulda thought of that before I drove up here. After two days of plush living, it's almost impossible to say no without feeling like a slob, an ingrate, and a rip-off artist.

I wonder how many married folk never wanted to be married in the first place? What if the day before the wedding they totted up the pros and cons one last time and the cons won? But you can't back out now! Good Lord, the invitations have been mailed, the caterer is planning to come, and what would the preacher think? How would you return the gifts you already received? And besides, you and Alphonse have "messed around a little." If you didn't want to be married to him, you should have thought of that before you did all that other stuff. D follows C, follows B, follows A! So you go ahead and marry. Maybe he'll work himself into an early grave; you can always "get it right" the next time.

When you've "made your bed" and now must lie in it, praying for a small, gentle miracle is the most you can do. Was there ever a person who, when considering the possibility of initiating a marital breakup, didn't want to avoid the responsibility? "Maybe he'll have an affair and leave me." "Maybe she'll go back to school in Montevideo." "Wouldn't it be terrible if a truck fell on him? . . . but then I wouldn't have to decide and I would *still* get out of it."

Not to beat a dead horse (Why do people say things like that when they clearly *intend* to beat a dead horse? Answer:

The message is, "I'm going to beat a dead horse, and I would appreciate your not mentioning the fact." Well, anyway—), during the Watergate finale, the nation slowly became aware of the outrages involved. Something had to be done, but impeachment was not the preferred choice. We would just have to learn to live with that pack of phonies. We elected them so we had to endure them for two more years. Fortunately, things got too bad to live with. It was only with the advent of "overwhelming evidence" that we were prepared, finally, to run them off.

Without getting into all the very real factors involved on both sides of the current abortion question, I'd like to mention that there is a gut-level conviction held by many who oppose abortions that the woman should have thought of the consequences before she "did it," as the euphemism goes. Now that she has "done it," she should pay the consequences. It occurs to me that the use of the word *pay* (or how about *suffer?*) indicates no small amount of revenge involved.

Hey! How about a corollary motto? "You must finish what you start!" People who don't finish things they start really get a bad press in our society. "He's a nice guy, but he never finishes what he starts." (Maybe they weren't worth finishing. Lots of things aren't worth the effort.) So we refer to those people as flighty and suspect they have a short attention span. Frequently, however, they are just terribly interested in many, many things.

I suffered for years from having to finish what I had started. Take reading, for example. Once I started a book I had to finish it, no matter how boring or trivial or repetitious or unrelated it was to anything that mattered to me. That included footnotes. A book was to be *read*. This was reinforced by my habit of keeping a record of "books I have read." I wouldn't record a book unless I had *finished* it. Since I'd "Made my bed" by opening the book, and because I wanted to add it to my list, I plowed through many a "junk" book. Especially if it was an "important" book. I take great pleasure these days in skimming books, re-reading the good ones, or reading outlines. My new goal is to enjoy and profit from my reading instead of finishing what I start.

American troops stayed in Vietnam long after the American public wanted out. Some said, though, "We have to stay because we started it." I loved the suggestion that we sneak all our forces out of Vietnam one dark night and leave a message behind declaring: THE WAR IS OVER AND WE WON.

Have you ever said, or been told to, clean your plate? I'll wager there isn't a kid in American who hasn't heard *and* said it. That phrase is as much a part of home life as "Jiggle the handle when you're through." Every Right-Thinking American knows that you just simply gotta clean your plate. Slipping some food to the dog doesn't count. The irony lies in the fact that usually the plate was dished up by someone else who ignored the desperate pleas of "Pulleeeze, not so much!"

We get accustomed to cleaning up plates that are dished up by others. The same is true of beds that others have made! "Yes, Sammy will take over the business when I retire. I've got him going to Flimflam U's School of Business now. He's kind of sad about not going into sociology but he'll get over that. Someday he'll thank me! (Sure, he will. With a twenty-foot tall grave marker, heavy enough to insure that the old man doesn't climb back out!)

I knew an air force chaplain who was obnoxious in a velvet-and-silk sort of way. He fought a lot, in militarily approved ways, with the staff sergeant assigned to assist him. One day the sergeant got sick and tired of the put-downs the officer passed out with such regularity. After a particularly disagreeable interchange, the sarge flung a mini-bomb: "Who called you into the ministry, chaplain? God, _____, or your, mother?" After several days of silence, the chaplain called the enlisted man into his office. "Sergeant, I want to thank you for what you asked. I've had three terrible days. You helped me realize that I became a minister to please my mother." He had never wanted to be a clergyman, and hated every minute of his work. He acted out his hatred by being obnoxious. I never heard what he did with that new information; I hope he took off like a big-nosed bird for happier stomping grounds.

Society makes lots of beds for others to sleep in. They are called roles. "Now that Sally's a mother, she can't go out much." "No, Sammy. We won't let you spend two years studying law. You're a plumber!" "We depend on you; the kids need college, and what about retirement and insurance? You can't change jobs." "We can't give you a charge account; you're a divorcee!"

This understanding that everything comes as a package deal makes the future seem inevitable and irreversible. Que sera, sera! Arthur Miller agreed when he has God say, in *Creation of the World and Other Business,* "You can never change the future. The past, yes, but not the future. . . . The past is always changing—nobody remembers anything. But the future can no more be turned away than the light flowing off the moon."

If the future has already been decided by the decisions we made yesterday, we cannot help but feel trapped if we don't like where we are today, or safe and secure within a false security, if we do. Sometimes, believing we've made all the right decisions, we are unprepared for changes that happen. One of the really sad lines from "All in the Family" came from Edith when she discovered that Archie had gone to another woman's apartment. "You were the one thing I could count on! And now I can't anymore."

More frequently, this sense of the inevitable future slams doors of possibility. Then we *have* to take what's coming to us. Once I watched a cat, Lucifer, that wanted to get into the

house. He was sitting outside a glass patio door, his path having led him to that particular spot. He was meowing loudly, demanding to be let in. The other sliding glass panel was wide open, only six inches to his left! But he wouldn't *look* to the left. He knew where he was and where he wanted to go. He was trapped unless something happened to help, such as somebody opening the door where he was. (Cats, I'm discovering, are dumb! Because they are so quiet we think them smart. "Any animal that quiet has got to be thinking!" We often think the same of some people.)

One night not long ago I saw a televised program on the plight of divorced people. One woman had been trying to get a job for two years, spending her days on the phone and in employment lines. She couldn't take shorthand and her typing was lousy; yet she applied mostly for jobs that required both. She was putting out a mammoth amount of energy. Nobody could fault her there. But I did yell at her through the TV set: "Go home and practice your typing!" The woman had tunnel-vision, like the cat. She didn't have to stay stuck. She could learn what she needed or change what she was looking for. She would do neither, however, as long as she stayed convinced that her plight was predetermined.

Remember when you were a kid and you learned to make some pretty funny faces, like pulling your mouth sideways with your fingers as far as it would stretch, then sticking your tongue way out? And maybe adding a "cross-eyed"? Another one was to pull your lower eyelids down with two fingers and push your nose up flat with a third. Just about the time you were really looking bizarre, someone would scream: "Don't *do* that! Your face will freeze!"

That "face will freeze" stuff gets said in many ways and supports one's conviction that "we've made our bed" permanently. Dad takes his daughter aside and explains that she shouldn't smile when boys flirt with her. "One thing always leads to another," he tells her. "And when you get to the *another* part, there you are!" Everyone seems certain that when you get to "there you are," you have to go ahead!

If this were true, then each decision we make *would* be superimportant. It would set off a long chain of unbreakable links, all leading relentlessly into the future. Once you decide, there would be no turning back. But in reality, that's only true if you're about to step off a six-hundred-foot cliff. Or such.

Remaking decisions that lead to a change for the better is further hindered by our fear of losing something important. There's an apt story in the New Testament to illustrate the point. The disciples of Jesus were out fishing for a living. After a long spell with no luck, they ran into a school of fish and caught 153 big ones, which is pretty good, even today. A man on shore had suggested the new spot. It suddenly dawned on them that the man giving the instructions was Jesus, whom they thought was dead. They really got excited! Peter, headstrong and headlong as usual, sprang into the sea in his eagerness to get to Jesus. The rest wanted to see him, too, but they couldn't bear to lose the fish he had helped them find, so they "came in the boat, dragging the net." Because they didn't want to lose their fish, they lost a rare and fantastic opportunity. They had baggage to carry.

If we try something new and it doesn't work, will we lose "some important fish"? This becomes a serious issue to people who want to grow. Few of us got everything "right" while growing up. I, for example, flunked being a kid. I was in such a hurry to grow up that I missed half of the things I could have learned along the way, such as how to chortle and giggle, how to be sad, how to play with other kids, and what to do when they didn't like me.

Some folk never have learned to accept attention; others never could separate themselves emotionally from their moms. Some never learned how to deal with their feelings.

Some missed the important information that it's OK to want to be alone sometimes. Many never had the chance to make their values fit the world they lived in. Some missed pieces from all of these areas, and if that happened, there is now only one solution: go back and do things over, only get them "right" this time. Not so long ago I went through a time of learning to let people hold me, during which time I discovered that I didn't have to *do* anything or pretend to be something *special*. I might have learned that a long time ago, but I didn't. When I finally learned that, my life took a big jump forward.

But we're not going to risk going back if we think our faces will freeze! Or that we will lose what we have. The voices from the cellars of our minds will scream, "Get off that floor, Herman! Do you want to spend your life acting like a two-year-old?" If Herman listens to that noise, he will refuse to act "like a two-year-old" and never learn what he needs to know about that age. If we want to develop a two-year-old talent, we have to get in touch with the part of us that will always be two years old. There's no danger we'll stay there; but we often feel as if there is, so we refuse to try it. Instead we choose to keep on keepin' on—the same old number as before.

Another thing that supports our "stuckness" is sympathy. Can you believe it? Sympathy, that act of commiserating with another person at a time of loss, can keep people stuck if they're not careful. The truly sympathetic person rejoices as loudly with a person's successes and joys as he cries over the failures. Most of us have difficulty doing the former.

There is an old story about a hermit who was above reproach. He could not be tempted in any fashion, but the Devil was determined to get him to mess up. He tempted the hermit with food and women, soft living opportunities and laziness, and all sorts of appeals. Nothing worked. He finally succeeded when he sent a fellow priest to the hermit's cave with news that the hermit's brother had just been promoted to bishop.

Crash! Jealousy and anger took over where nude ladies had failed. I point this out to show we tend to have trouble being sympathetic with success. Sympathizing, however, comes easily when someone is hurting more than we are. If you listen you can hear a lot of "poor baby!" phrases in use. People who like each other want to be understanding, so they sympathize easily with each other and accept "what had to be." The more we get "good strokes" for lying in the "bed we made," the more likely we are to figure out how to stay there and make ourselves more comfortable. We learn to "put up with it."

Don't misunderstand. Sympathy is good. I just don't want to get "hooked" on it. When I fall down and skin my knee, I *want* someone to hold me and maybe even dry my tears. But then I want to get on with what I was doing. I *don't* want to go shopping for a cane.

There is only one possible application of the phrase "You've made your bed, now lie in it!" I think the motto has a kernel of truth that could be said in a better fashion. How about, "Every event has consequences that must be dealt with." I find it useful to remember that I "signed up" for whatever happened. A young friend of mine refuses to sympathize with football players who break an arm or leg while playing. He's quick to mention that they've been out there practicing all week just for the chance to do something that frequently breaks limbs. Whining when you get what you asked for is a waste of energy. If we smoke three packs of "coffin nails" a day for thirty years, it isn't amazing that our lungs give out. We have indeed "made our bed" and we will indeed "lie in it." When you think about it, that's how people use this motto—they want the whining to stop!

Every decision we make has consequences and those consequences frequently involve other people. This means they will, of necessity, be involved to some degree in how the issues are resolved. If we choose to ignore both the conse-

quences of our decisions and the people involved in them, we will end up invariably worse off than before.

Yet I'm in favor of dumping the whole slogan! Telling people that they have made their beds and we're all tickled to death that they get to suffer the consequences is not helpful. It's sadistic! Telling *yourself* that is stupid. I find it much more useful simply to remind myself, "That's what happens when you play football." Now I'm free to accept the consequences in good grace or decide that I won't play football anymore. (I've been in one honest-to-God fistfight in my life. Eighth grade, with Dick Fleming. He was a nice guy so he took it easy on me; but I hurt enough to make some radical decisions about the value of beating on someone else and getting myself beaten on. I haven't regretted the decision one iota!)

This motto doesn't allow for personal growth *or* external changes. It hinders people from recognizing that they can re-decide any time they want. "Today is the first day of the rest of my life," as Dag Hammarskjöld said.

Even our bodies change as we grow. I've often thought of taking "before and after" pictures of people in therapy, as orthodontists do with their dental patients. As we change our thinking, we change the way we look and act, too.

As we grow older, experience more things, and learn more about our life and our world, we do change a lot. Trying to stay the same is probably one of the most illogical and impossible things we can try. Once you've been a parent, you'll never think like a nonparent again. Once you've been to school, you can't ever act or feel unschooled again. You can merely try to fake it! Once you've been to Paris, the farm won't ever look the same. It might even look better, but it *will* look different.

Turning loose of the past, of once made beds, is not as horrendous as it feels. Making sizeable change always produces stress that must be dealt with. Remaking beds requires energy, but it doesn't necessarily produce the sense of loss and defeat and of things being wasted that usually keeps us from taking action.

What about giving up a career, a marriage, a life-style or a homestead? When I left the air force after ten years' active duty, I realized I hadn't wasted a thing! Those years are still precious to me. Much of what I am today came from the happenings during those ten years. My tunic still fits, so I can put it on from time to time and recall the feeling that comes with it. I constantly use the lessons I learned about people, organizations, other-faith groups, tragic death, and so on.

Nothing is ever lost! And nothing is wasted, unless we refuse to use what we gained from our experiences. In college, my primary studies were in philosophy. I can't think of any degree more nonsalable than one in philosophy. It is worthless on the market, unless you have a doctorate and can be hired as a college professor. But if I had it to choose over, I'd choose the same major. I didn't waste those years by any stretch of the imagination. I learned a whole new way of thinking and of viewing life. A degree in philosophy probably reflects closest to pure education.

Since nothing of our past can be lost, we are free much of the time to make new decisions. Some things can't be redecided, like jumping off cliffs or cutting off legs, but other issues can be. One of the larger schools of Transactional Analysis, founded by Bob and Mary Goulding, bases its therapeutic work on the conviction that we behave as we do because we decided to do so. Either recently or a long time ago we decided to work hard, or be lonely, or feel depressed, or not be successful, or whatever. Almost every aspect of our lives can be traced back to some decision we made. As we take responsibility for having made those decisions, we are free to redecide them.

We can decide to begin asking for what we want. We can make new decisions about how we get people to pay attention to us. We can redecide almost anything. I am becoming more certain as the years go by that when people decide to change, they do change! Across the board. Remember the old saying, "Where there's a will there's a way"? I'm convinced that's true. Once I've decided—really decided—to do something, I will figure out a way to get that done. If I've decided and still don't change, another decision is blocking the way.

The Fangschleister family wants to be a happy family and is failing. Dad F. says, "We've decided we're going to be happy, but we're not. So you're wrong, Art Greer!" Let's look at that. How they are staying unhappy has to do with decisions they've made. They have decided that happy families bowl together, so they whip off to the lanes every chance they get, always together. Three of the four don't particularly *like* what they're doing. They've decided togetherness is the key to happiness, so they do *everything* together, including some pretty private things. They've decided that happy families live in neat places, so they nag and holler at each other when something is out of place. They've decided that happy families eat the evening meal at six, together, and other schedules be damned. They fight a lot, trying to get everyone to eat together.

They haven't decided to be happy! They have really decided to be neat, to be together always, to do things they don't want to do, and to try to eat together. These are the real decisions. Once they decide the *main* issue, and give up those decisions which block the way, they *will* be happy. Not before.

They may decide to give up some of their cluttering habits but stay comfortable with a little mess. Each may decide to take more time alone. They might plan family meals to fit the schedules of those involved. Abraham Lincoln said, "Most people are as happy as they've a mind to be." I can't emphasize that enough.

You are doing what you've decided to do! By paying attention to what you actually *do,* you can quickly get in touch with what you've decided and spot the things that need changing. When the Fangschleisters decide that happiness is their number one priority, they will change a lot of behaviors to get there. We get stuck when the real decision is, "I won't be happy until *you*. . . ." St. Paul said he had decided to be content in whatever situation he found himself. Good for him!

Please be aware that I'm *not* talking about remaking your bed every morning. Redeciding things every time you get the urge could become fairly tedious, too. But you don't have to wait until the sheets rot before you make your bed so that you sleep well.

7

Even the Sphinx Lost His Nose

THEY ALL LIVED HAPPILY EVER AFTER

One of life's curses is that (for some strange reason) we always seem to be so preoccupied with the "urgent" that we don't take time to do the "important." Like setting goals! Whether we like it or not, one of the most important needs we have is Goal-Setting. It is difficult to get experience at goal-setting because until we are fairly well along in years (somewhere between fifteen and ninty-three, depending on our cultural environment) somebody else provides the goals. "You gotta go to school, and here's what you're gonna take." Even our extracurricular activities seem designed by someone else. "Everybody's joining the band." "We're all going to Schultz's for beer." "Nobody would date *her*."

We are told the fashionable things to wear, to do, and to think. We are told that a kid who won't go to college is flunking being a human and isn't living up to his potential. No choice—we go! Raising kids well has sometimes been a goal for thousands of parents who really didn't want kids in the first place. Know anyone whose goal is to retire? (I want to write a book on retirement some day. Retirement has to be the dumbest goal in the world unless you're prepared to do it right now!)

Lots of people marry because someone else thought they should be married. How about the goal of having a cabin in the woods or a little chicken farm? Have you ever known anyone who wanted one, got it, and liked it? For every one that did, I'll wager there are 348 who didn't like it. They got out there but then yearned for the life they used to have. Same with a lot of Florida retirements, I'll bet.

If we pursue goals that others have set for us, we don't get much practice at setting our own. I think many of us have a goal that we decided to pursue as children and that we still stalk relentlessly. "To live happily ever after." To find the Disneyland, where everything is in place and we have finally put life all together once and for all. This magic scenario will occur when the last dragon has been slain and the final witch has been banished into the dark woods forever. Then we also will have a hot line to the Wizard of Oz!

I refuse to believe that we can listen to so many fairy tales without coming to understand that the goal in life is to live happily every after, just like the prince and princess. Someone suggested to me that this was not a slogan followed by grown-ups. I disagree. I've never met a person who wasn't convinced that it is possible to "nail life down," once and for all. I am amazed, astounded and confounded every time my car's engine starts sputtering its desire for a tune-up. Despite all the evidence to the contrary—despite my awareness that this is a natural and expected event—a part of me is *always* outraged. "I just had it tuned up ten thousand miles ago. What in hell does it want this time? Will it never be satisfied?" I do the same when light bulbs go bad or the sewer line gets infested with tree roots again.

It's my hunch that when we long for the beach house, or retirement, a part of us is picturing a destination where we can stay forever, filled with only Ups, and no Downs in sight. At a cosmic level, the farm house with a few chickens becomes "sitting on a cloud, playing a harp while God smiles down." I think Heaven was designed by folk who gave up on this life and decided it might happen there.

Let me take you on a side path to throw light on my main point. The biblical story of Adam and Eve is a magnificent one. Unfortunately, I think its main ideas have been badly interpreted by a majority of those who tell bible stories. In the popular press, Adam and Eve are given a really square deal by a loving God. Then they promptly foul up by refusing to follow the dorm rules. God, sly old man, had planted a tree in the middle of their existence to test them. (God, as many describe him, sounds like a frustrated educational psychologist who adores testing people, and flunking them. Breast cancer is not a disease; the woman simply is being "tested." As nearly as I can tell, if she complains about her condition she will flunk. A "good person" will, when a tree falls on his back, sing "We're Marching to Zion" instead of yelling "Ouch, %#¢$&* it!" But I digress. Back to the garden.)

Adam and Eve flunk the test when they eat some of the juicy, succulent fruit of that tree, for in doing so they discover their genitalia. Having found them, they decide to put them to use, and being clever, they also figure out a way to connect them, thereby sealing their fate. God immediately leaps from behind a bush, crying "Aha!" He has suspected all along that they were going to cheat. He throws them out of paradise and punishes them by making Adam work for a living, Eve to menstruate and hurt during childbirth, the snake to lose his feet and legs to remind him of his part in the treachery.

God, according to this perverted translation, refuses to be content with his punishment of Adam and Eve, so he causes their "sinfulness" to be passed on to everyone else in the world, apparently through ova and sperm. You and I are supposed to catch hell for their mistakes, too.

I am not making light of the garden of Eden story. It is an

important, accurate description of a large part of our existence. I'm spoofing the long-held, third grade *interpretation* of the story. Let me tell my understanding of this great myth.

We have all been to the garden of Eden. For roughly nine months we experienced the perfect existence, and the memory of our days in the womb is imbedded in our brains and our bodies. All things were provided for us, without labor on our part. Our every need was met. The temperature was constant, the food was piped directly into our stomachs, we didn't have to breathe or swallow, nor did our eyes have to deal with the vagaries of light. It was Eden. And then came the earthquakes and the flood.

With birth came the end of Eden and the impossibility of returning. To become human we had to give up our perfect existence and assume the not-so-perfect requirements of humanity, like work and menstrual periods, survival and autonomy. Unprotected by our mother's womb, we put on fig leaves and, later, took them off to procreate. We have had to endure the pain of watching our sons kill one another and suffer the penalty of being fugitives and wanderers on Earth.

This wonderful myth is loaded with man's earliest insights into our existential problems and of what it means to be human. Adam and Eve's problem was *not* that they were evil, wretched ingrates; their problem, like ours, was that they had become *humans*. The tree from which our first parents ate was the tree of "the knowledge of good and evil." Knowing the difference between good and evil, they no longer *could* remain in Eden. If God hadn't thrown them out, they would have walked out on their own, saying, "This ain't good for *us!*"

I am convinced that we do have the memory of Eden within us, and the memory urges us to return. Church dogma tells us there is a new Eden, now called Heaven. Social dreamers speak of, and design, places they refer to as utopias. Even B. F. Skinner, a pragmatic psychologist, has designed "Walden

Two" based on behavior modification. Accustomed to persuading rats to run where he wants them to run, he is convinced that people can be persuaded to act similarly. I don't wish him well. I don't think it can be done, but if it can I will fight it. Hitler had a similar idea of controlling human behavior.

Some folk have become disillusioned with the promise of Utopia. Life's negative blows have persuaded them to give it *all* up, so they flee to the other end of the spectrum with a firm resolution never to be happy. "Life is not to be enjoyed," they report, "it is to be endured." This sort of decision is made quite frequently. If life isn't white then it must be black. There's no middle ground. That's a good way to stay in trouble, too.

Yet despite our memories and our dreams, our exile from Eden is real and permanent. Even the Sphinx succumbed to "reality" by losing his nose to the sands of time and the winds of change. The faucets will need new washers no matter what I do. When the kids get one phase of their lives in order, they will enter another with a whole new set of demands. I'll bet even Clark Gable had days when he didn't feel much like a star, and said so as he headed for the aspirin. When we reach a goal that is expected to eliminate distress, remove disliked chores, and give us Eden, we are always disappointed. An air force sergeant told me about the time he was standing in the coffee line at a Pentagon snack bar, a cigar box full of empty cups in his hand. Suddenly he noticed two stars on the shoulder of the man behind him. He stepped aside immediately and asked the major general to go ahead of him. "Stay where you are, sarge!" chuckled the general, who also held a box full of cups. "I'm the junior man in my office, too!"

This is why all of our attempts to Settle Down result in some sort of failure. No matter how many roots we sink, we find our lives are still like canoes on the Mississippi River. At best the roots are anchors that give momentary stability. From time to time the anchors drag from the pull of the current and we have to find new places to set them. Helen Keller said, "Life is either a daring adventure or it is nothing," and I agree with her. Growth and change are critical ingredients of life. I don't know whether we *ought* to change and grow—I only know that we *shall*. The question is how? In what direction?

Some folk grow up, others out, and some like Topsy—in whatever direction. Some grow in weird ways and blame it on fate or their parents. Some grow and pretend they don't. Some grow backwards, in a sort of negative growth pattern. But we *all* grow. I figure that if we gotta grow, it might as well be in a direction we like. To do that requires that we accept the fact of growth and change. It also means accepting the things that go with change, such as disturbance and discomfort.

It has been helpful to me to see life as if it happened on a sailing vessel. Some things stay the same from day to day, like the deck, the hatches, and the rails. Other things, like the sails, are reasonably constant but do change from time to time. But the waters through which we travel, and the winds that push us, are constantly changing and must be reckoned with. Neither is an annoyance to the true adventurer. If either element disappears, the boat and its people are in bad trouble. The winds and the waters are necessities to sailing.

Some days the boat sails along calmly; on others, because of heavier seas, it will pitch, roll on its beam-ends, and then snap back. With a quartering sea, or running before the wind, it may yaw if the helmsman does not keep the sheets properly trimmed. When winds are high, so are the seas, which send spray over the bow to slap your face.

Life has such variance. There is nothing wrong with enjoying "balmy days and quiet seas," but to expect them to last forever is a setup for disappointment. There is nothing wrong with avoiding storms and high waves, but the boat is going to *move* in all but the quietest seas. And movement means disturbance. One of the biggest disturbances when we change is the reaction of the people around us.

One story that always sets me laughing is the account of Jesus' recruitment of Matthew, a tax collector, as one of his disciples. Passing by, he said to him, "Follow me." "And he rose and followed him." (It isn't in italics in the Bible, but it should be, with seventeen exclamation points after it.) Stop and consider for a moment the nine kinds of hell this little scene raised. It helps explain why the establishment wanted Jesus gone permanently. Matthew was a tax collector, GS-7. While pious eyes may only see his faithful response, anyone who has ever worked for the government *knows* the response of Matthew's supervisor, GS-13, when he got the word that the tax office was abandoned and the money box unguarded (and perhaps even stripped). Did he remember to sign the IRS form 605 for the day? Can't you see the pen still chained to the desk, the door wide open, the fan still running? I imagine the government declared Matthew an irresponsible, flighty individual in its termination form 931. Sometimes our goals take us in directions that others see as irresponsible or flighty. When they do, we will hear about it. You can expect the supervisors will make strange noises.

You may not like the ground rules, but this seems to be the only game in town: Growth and Change and Disturbance and sometimes Discomfort. You ain't *ever* going to live Happily Ever After. Sorry.

Given that, in which direction do you want to head? Some people decide to just move out and see what might come along that is of interest to them. Most of us, though, will prefer to choose a goal.

The key factor is *intention*. "I intend to do something." The "stopper" comes when we add the additional clause, "but I haven't decided yet what it is I *want*." Simply wanting to move might produce some activity, but the action will be unfocused and abstract. Like the moth, whose only intention seems to get close to a light, we will fly to the nearest light (usually the brightest) and stay there for a spell. If the light goes off, or we get bored, then off we go to whatever light is next or nearer. We can cover a lot of territory that way, but we will wear ourselves out and there will be little direction to what we do. Sometimes our simple intention to go to the next bright spot "gets us dead," as the moth finds out when he flies into the electrified moth catcher.

The moth does what we call mindless activity. He doesn't think much about his life, he just gets on with it. If that's what the moth really wants, he's in a good place. I've met very few people who are content to drift through life. Most of us have some fairly concrete ideas of what we don't want, and drifting is one of them. Knowing what we don't want helps, but not much. Remember the great movie *Marty* and its fine portrayal of indecision? "What do you want to do tonight, Marty?" "I don't know. What do you want to do?" Every idea would get vetoed. Thirty-five wrong ideas later they were still saying, "What do *you* want to do!" My hunch is that they *really* wanted to stay home and talk to each other about doing something.

Indecision is a horrible thing for most of us unless we've firmly decided *not* to decide. People with a terminal case of it (like Marty) found out as kids that they were not supposed to be doing whatever they were doing. "Mom sent me to find out what you were doing and tell you to quit it!" Their big Road Map guideline is *don't*. If they do decide to do something, they immediately wish they hadn't. "I should be studying." "I probably should be taking a rest instead of fixing this light switch." "I'll bet the other movie was better." To "not decide" is to condemn yourself to a lifetime of wobbling.

There are two kinds of goals, long-term and short-term. The former are called strategies and the latter, tactics. The first one happily comes first. One way of choosing an overall, long-term strategy for life is to lie down on the couch and pretend you're going to be dead in an hour. Go back over your life. What are the things you are really pleased for having done? What are the things you *missed,* the missing of which makes you go *Awwwwwww?* What are the things you wish you hadn't spent so much time on? What is it you want to say about your life when it is all over? (The best some folk will be able to say is that they never went out without their umbrella!) Will that statement be worth a lifetime? Doing that kind of thinking, it doesn't take too long before you get some idea of the kind of strategy you want for your life, and what new long-time goals you want.

Once the strategy is settled, determining the tactics, or short-term goals, is far easier. What are some things you are going to do or deal with or get settled or experience during the next few months that lead toward your larger goal? I think painting the house is a worthwhile operation, but it falls short of the kind of tactics I have in mind unless your strategy is to leave things better than you find them. Tactics are concrete ways we can begin to realize our long-term goals *right away.*

I like to urge people to retire now! I'm not suggesting that they quit earning money, but I am convinced that it is a mistake to put off *anything* important until some far-off, future date. If playing shuffleboard in St. Petersburg is truly important to you, then I suggest figuring out a way to do that while you can still see the other court. You might not *want* to do it twenty-five years from now. I know many folk who have really neat, concrete plans for spending their years as senior citizens. Let's say it includes building a potting shed to grow rare flowers. My hunch is that if they put it off until they "quit work," they won't enjoy it when they get the chance. Happily retired people spend their time doing what they've *always* enjoyed doing, only more of it. So work it into your life now! If it's something you really want, you can build your retirement joy in the next eight weeks—if you want to.

Setting goals isn't all that hard, unless you fall into some pitfalls along the way. I've gotten in touch with four pitfalls that frequently keep people from living happily for even the next six months.

The first two pitfalls of Goal-Setting are fairly straightforward. *Confusing short-term and long-term goals.* A quick way to "not get where you want" is to turn a short-term goal into a lifetime operation. I did that with book writing. "Some day, I'm gonna write a book." Want a dollar for every person who has said that? I had been a journalist in college and had written a thousand short pieces that ranged from newspaper variety columns to sermons. I knew I could write and I enjoyed it. Someday. . . . Believe it or not, writing a book is a *short-term goal!* At least for me. It was something I could do anytime I decided to get my act together. So is moving to the country, going to work for yourself, going to work (if you are a work-all-day-at-home-woman, and therefore don't "work") or getting a college degree. So is building an addition to the house, visiting the Ozarks, and reading *War and Peace.*

I see long-term, strategic goals as the umbrella under which these shorter goals fit, such as experiencing as many different things as I can, or creating an even balance between work (which is something I don't especially want to do) and play (which is something I would pay for the chance to do) or learning something new twice a week. Such as learning as much as I can about one particular subject or learning something about as many things as I can. Or deciding to be potent in almost every situation. Or being either a people-oriented person or a thing-oriented one. Long-term goals describe in reasonably complete detail what we will have done when we come to the end of our lives. Short-term goals describe the particular ways we get there.

The second pitfall on the way to goal-setting is *refusing to use contracts,* both as we begin to plan and along the way. A contract is a well-defined, concrete spelling out of what's going to happen, and who does what, and probably when. Can you picture the problems you would have if you shopped without a contract? (Some folk do, but you have to be *rich* to get away with it!) "Send some kind of stove over will you?" "Sure, we'll do that sometime." "About how much will it cost?" "Oh, we'll let you know." "OK!" You can already see the troubles that are coming.

We wouldn't *shop* that way, but a lot of us are happily prepared to *live* that way. Then we wonder why we can't even see Disneyland on the horizon, let alone get there. Transactional analysis is a contractual psychotherapy, so we make a lot of contracts. "What do you want out of therapy?" "Oh," say a lot of clients, "I want to be happier." Or, "I want to like myself better." Well," says the therapist, "how will you be acting differently when you're feeling happier?" Usually the client looks at the therapist as if *she's* the one who needs treatment. Frequently, the answer is: "I'll know when I get there." We haven't been trained to plan our way to what we want. We'll just know when it happens (if it does). Once the contract is narrowed down, a way to proceed becomes clearer. "I will be smiling more and not tensing up my muscles. I won't be working at the time." Now the person can explore why he does not want to smile or to quit working all the time, and how he decides to stay tense. It's fine to decide to go "somewhere," but you're *already* "somewhere." If you are going to move, you have to decide what that new somewhere is going to look like in concrete terms.

After drawing up a contract with yourself that describes your plan, one last step is required. Take a hard look at the possibilities. Is the contract *feasible*? Lots of folk make contracts they cannot possibly keep. "Yes, Myrtle, I promise never to look at another woman as long as I live!" A setup for failure. Any contract that has an *always* or a *never* in it is probably doomed. A deaf-mute will probably fail as a music critic or an actor. Given my weight and skeletal make-up, deciding to avoid football was a smart move on my part. There aren't enough shoulder and thigh-pads in the *world* to keep me alive at that for long. Heading for the garden of Eden falls in the same category, unless you're willing to shoot heroin and die quickly.

The other side of the coin is shooting too low. Some folk set goals they could easily surpass. They settle for half. Usually we decide to aim low because we are discounting our abilities and talents. Lyndon Johnson explained that any time a bill of his successfully passed in the Senate by a large number of votes, he knew he hadn't put as many things as he might have into it! He always asked for the most he could get.

The third pitfall is a little more complicated; *be sure to pick a Loser's way of operating.* Eric Berne, the founder of Transactional Analysis, was much interested in what he called Life Scripts. A Life Script is the program we adopt early in life that describes where we are going and how we are going to get there. He wanted to know what made the difference between Winners and Losers. How do some people maintain a winning life-style while others are content to be Frogs (Losers) sitting on a lily pad saying, "Ribbitt, Ribbitt"? ("Ribbitt" is our explanation of why we have a *right* to be Losers: "If only my boss were more understanding. . . ." or "My wife won't *let* me be more outgoing." Ribbitt.)

Berne spent a lot of time analyzing Frog Scripts. In his book *What Do You Say After You Say "Hello"?,* he described six of them. For each type, he found a figure from ancient mythology to illustrate the pattern that produces a Loser.

Berne called the first one the *Always Script.* Arachne, having displeased the goodess Athena, was brought back from the dead and condemned to spend the rest of her time as a spider, endlessly weaving and spinning webs. Some folk's lives are like that. Their tombstones could well read, "She never quit cooking." "He was always fixing something." "He was always running from bar to bar."

An air force chaplain told me of his assignment to the National Cemetery at Arlington, Virginia. He conducted about four funerals a day. He had lots of unusual stories to tell. One was of a master sergeant's wife who refused to leave when he handed her the folded flag at the end of the graveside services. He stayed with her until the mourners left then tried again to budge her, with no success. Still the answer was no, so together they watched the men fill the grave, cover it with sod, re-arrange the flowers and tamp down the grave. Finally she said, "OK, chaplain, I'm ready to leave." As they walked slowly to the limousine, she turned toward him and said with evident calm, "You know, this will be the first night in thirty-three years . . . that I will know where that son-of-a-bitch is!" She could have chiseled Always Running on his tombstone.

In the Walt Disney version of the story, Cinderella *always* sat in the ashes and did the dirty work, singing "Someday My Prince Will Come" to amuse herself. In the story he did come. In life, he seldom does; the fairy godmother forgets to send him.

Another type of Life Program is the opposite of the one above and Berne called it the *Never Script.* Its hero is Tantalus (from whose name we get the word "tantalize.") Though the son of a god himself, he was such a wretch that he was condemned to be chained to a wall while surrounded with innumerable good things like food and ladies. (According to another account, he was suspended from a fruit tree over a pond. When he bent to drink, the water would recede. When he reached for fruit, the wind would blow it beyond his reach.) People with Never Scripts live lives of avoidance. They deny themselves anything pleasurable. If something comes up, they carefully schedule conferences to conflict, or have migraine headaches. They are not worthy of enjoyment. They have instructions stored in the back of their heads that read "never be happy," "never trust men/women," "never like yourself," or "never relax."

A third program for failure is the *Until Script* with Jason as the model. Jason had to do a lot of scary and hard things before he was allowed to assume his rightful place as king. (Jacob, son of Isaac, had the same problem when he had to work seven years to get the girl he wanted, was tricked into marrying her older sister, and had to put in another seven before he got what he wanted.) People with this script know that someday they will get to live their own lives, but in the meantime their lives belong to others. "Oh, I couldn't do that. My family comes first." "I won't get married; my mother needs me." "My heart belongs to mamma, my soul belongs to God, and my arse belongs to the company." People who are going to do it all after retirement belong in this category.

The *After Script* follows Damocles, the fellow who was the guest of honor at a banquet. Above his head was a huge sword suspended by a thread. His host wanted him to recognize the fragility of power and the ever-present nature of great danger. People following this plan for living are allowed to enjoy what they are doing to some degree, but they are sure it is only temporary. Someday, down the road, the sword will fall and they must then give up their power and turn into Frogs. For some the sword never falls, but their lives have been diluted by their excessive fear of tomorrow. For others, the sword falls when they marry or have their first child. Some delightful women turn into Frogs when they reach thirty, "knowing" they have lost their youth and charm. For others the magical year is forty, or forty-five, and the sword is "middlescent-senility." I have known men to suddenly take to twin beds and abandon their sex lives because "it was time."

Have you ever seen people begin acting old almost over-night? An eighty-year-old once commented about her overly middle-aged children. "If I hang around much longer, they're going to be old before I am."

The fifth pattern for Losers is the *Over-and-Over Script.* Sisyphus was the mythological guy who was given just one task—rolling a huge boulder up a hill. When he got it there, he could quit. As fate would have it, just as he had it *almost* to the top, the damned thing would roll back down to the bottom. It didn't take too many of those in a row before even Sisyphus got the picture. Someone powerful was out to get him, and he would most likely spend eternity with that miserable marble. These scripts are similar to the *Always Script,* except that they are cyclical. Instead of falling like the quick, repetitious jerks of a jackhammer, the repetitions become apparent only after long periods of time. A man goes to work for a company, climbs the corporate ladder, and manages to "get in trouble" halfway up. He joins another company and repeats the whole process. From beginning to end, many different events occur, but the overall pattern is exactly the same. Some people do the same thing with marriages. Others with friends.

Finally, Berne described the *Open-ended Script.* Such a script is really only halfway planned. It goes fairly well up to some point and then fades away. The person is left with a sec-ond half that is "planless." Philemon and Baucis were a husband-and-wife team in mythology. When they "got it right," they were rewarded by being turned into trees, she into a laurel, he into an oak. The fact that their branches inter-twined was supposed to make it even nicer. Some people have fine Life Programs; the only hitch is that the program is dependent on something outside themselves, like job or chil-dren. When the external world changes, their plan is through whether *they* like it or not. Women whose lives center around the children frequently find themselves at a loss when the children leave home or rebel against having another's life totally centered on them. Men whose only real joy is the job have little to do when retirement comes but count the rocks on the rocking chair and wait for death.

Poor Alexander the Great gave up and died at thirty-three. He was fine so long as he had a new world to conquer. When he ran out of "worlds," he ran out of gas. It never occurred to him to try something new. These are open-ended (unfinished) scripts.

These are the major programs for Frogs (or Losers):
1. Always the same old thing.
2. Never getting what I want.
3. Gotta keep at it until I. . . .
4. Staying just ahead of disaster.
5. Go back and start over again.
6. Everything's fine if nothing changes.

Winners have programs that let them win now *and* later regardless of what happens outside them.

A fourth pitfall keeps us from setting adequate, satisfying goals. It is concerned with the degree of our involvement with other people. We are always in some sort of tension between the horns of *autonomy* and *security*.

On the one hand, we all want some degree of security and to be a part of some community. Why else would there be so many organizations? When I was on the University of Houston campus we had 247 different organizations! There must have been one for Grass Watchers. I'm sure there was one for Grass Smokers, given the times. And those were just the *recognized* organizations.

You don't really need an organization to accomplish most of the deeds that are the result of organized groups. Nine out of ten organizations don't get all that much *done,* in my experience. So why are there so many organizations? And so many organizers? To paraphrase, "They're the kind of people who, if you like that kind of people, you'd like." Organizations bring folk together around some central theme so they can belong—together. And that's nice. St. Paul said, "None of us lives by himself, and none of us dies by himself." I think that's true. (If any of my readers thinks it might be arrogant to differ, or foolish to agree, with such an august person as Paul, I would point out that you don't have to quit arguing with someone just because he got published, and that includes me.)

We are surrounded by people, and with the population exploding, our chances of living or dying alone are decreasing. The Big Question for many folk today is, "How do I find the opportunity to be autonomous and to make my own decisions in this crowded, mechanized world?" While John Donne's statement "No man is an island" has a lot of truth to it, many of us want to be at least peninsulas! We want to be free and independent, and able to choose our own courses. Consequently, there is a massive surge throughout our American society toward "aloneness." I suspect we have found more security than we wanted in the first place. Big Government, Big Labor, Big Church, Big Apartment Complex, Big Supermarket, not to mention Big Insurance Plans, Social Security, Big Universities, and Big Medicine, cannot help but give the impression that we are *surrounded*. Is Big Brother next? Some folk think so and have formed yet another organization to watch for him. You can even buy a computerized date selection if you want; you don't even have to *look* for a mate!

I suspect that the age of the Big Everything partly explains the drive toward autonomy we are currently witnessing. Ten years ago, apartment houses had taken over 25 percent of Houston. I'll bet the figure is closer to 50 percent by now. A huge majority of those areas is occupied by single people or single people living together. Singles clubs are busy and popular. Singles bars are growing. The swing toward autonomy is in full operation. If you want it done "right," do it yourself!

With that swing comes loneliness and sometimes great difficulties. I like to do things for myself. But if I want it done "right," I am *not* going to rely on me if I ever get appendicitis! I like baking oatmeal cookies; but thank God for the guys who produce the oatmeal. A man who defends himself in court, as the saying goes, "has a fool for a lawyer and an idiot for a client." Only last week the papers reported just such a case. The guy finally "ripped his knickers" while cross-examining his victim. He asked, "With the light so dim, are you sure you got a good look at my face when I took your purse?"

To avoid this pitfall, it is important to get some balance between autonomy and community. Some people decide never to leave the fold. They cling, like younger brothers, to anyone who can do something for them. They wouldn't brush their own teeth if they could find a volunteer. (If I were God of the whole school system, I would have every junior high boy taking home economics so he could cook, bake, and sew for himself. Every junior high girl would be required to take shop so she could use tools and fix things for herself. There is no reason for people to eat burnt eggs or stir paint with a screwdriver after twelve years of schooling!)

Other people swing all the way toward autonomy and never make it back. They go through life screaming, "Mother, I want to do it for myself." If they know how to do something, they won't *let* someone else do it. A person like this generally ends up marrying the helpless clinger.

There is no utopia, but we can build something reasonably similar. We begin by nailing down what is good and important and real to *us* and giving up the goals someone *else* pawned off on us. Disneyland would get boring after a week anyway!

8

Someday My Ship Will Come In

EVERYTHING COMES TO HIM WHO WAITS

One evening, while working a jigsaw puzzle with my son, a senior in high school, I was listening to him tell me about things he could hardly wait for, such as the arrival of his letter jacket, a specially made patch signifying his participation in the parade of tall ships during the bicentennial, and his real driver's license.

After a pregnant pause, he remarked, "It isn't as if life were passing me by. I'm just waiting for it to *get* here!" I recalled how impossibly difficult waiting can be, especially for teen-agers with things to do on their minds—graduation, college, steady girl- or boyfriends, summer trips, places of their own in the world. Teen-agers have a tough time of it and ought to be given a lot of leeway, I think.

Waiting is small joy for many of us, and the old motto "Anticipation is half the fun" somehow fails to carry the burden of waiting. While I am a very patient man when it comes to threading needles or other such delicate operations, I am the world's worst waiter. I would *far* rather miss a good movie or see it much later than stand in a long line waiting to get in. If there is a line for Heaven, I will happily go to Hell. (If you listen to some people, all my friends will be there anyway.)

Since there are a lot of things to wait for in this life, impatient kids have to learn about waiting. Society has a banner motto for just such a case: "Everything comes to him who waits." (Her, too, presumably.) Didn't you hear that expression a few times while you were crawling the wall because Christmas was coming so slowly? Has any reader not heard the phrase, "Patience, my child!" while sitting in the back seat of the family sedan and screaming for the thirty-ninth time, "Aren't we *there* yet?" In our eagerness to get ice-cream cones we were told, "Wait your turn." Wanting to see something that society had decided was only for grown-ups we were told, "Wait until you are eighteen." We couldn't use dad's electric drill because we were supposed to "wait until you're a big boy or girl." Oh, the wondrous things we were going to do someday, when. . . . Well, "Rome wasn't built in a day!"

I can't find it among my memorabilia, but somewhere I have a cutting from *David Blaze of Kings,* a book I read as a kid. I loved it, because it captured so well the idea of waiting for life to "get here." Each time the hero finished a phase of his life he found out it was only the beginning. After a lifetime in school, he attended a commencement and was told that he could now begin the Real Life. When he married, he could begin to seek the Real Life of parenthood. On and on. Lying on his deathbed, he was solemnly informed by his priest that this life was but a shadow of the Real Life beyond. At death he could *really* begin. In great physical and mental agony, he screamed, "Great God, haven't I begun yet?" whereupon, said the writer, he died and went straight to Hell.

A life of waiting is a bummer; yet there are few of us who have not been taught that everything comes to him who waits Some of us have learned to become Professional Waiters who have turned waiting into a fine art. The all-time champion was a man in the Bible who laid beside a pool in Bethsaida waiting for an angel to trouble the water. He made a career out of waiting! Thirty-eight years!

Webster declares that waiting means to be in a state of expectation. We know how to be expectant! We look forward to marriage, children, retirement, Christmas, vacations, and trips, and some of us to divorce. We anticipate new wardrobes and cars. We hope for good friends and a better job. We bide time until we get to upper management and move to the nice part of town. We mark time until the next birthday, book, or annual conference. We wait until we're seniors; on our own; free from hassles; we wait to find someone to understand us, and for the ten o'clock news.

There is a good side to learning to wait. Some things *have* to be waited for. Most babies take nine months or so to get ready for birth. All the activity in the world won't get them ready any sooner. Same with time-in-grade for promotions, the mail delivery of the United States postal service, and twelve hours by the clock. It takes a certain amount of time for water to boil or for ideas to sink into our heads. Pushing the River (to use Fritz Perl's terminology once more) is a sheer waste of time. Did you ever watch a kid watching a plant grow? I know one who reported actually pulling the plant out of the ground to make sure the roots were taking hold.

My point is that we can learn the lesson of waiting *too well*! While some people rush in where angels fear to tread, most of us have learned to stand and wait until we're *pushed*. In the words of Jonathan Livingston Seagull, "We dream while we wait . . ." and pray ". . . Dear Father." Waiting can become a Life-Style. I remember hearing of a relative who frequently said that he was waiting for his ship to come in. He killed a lot of time "walking down to the harbor" to see if it had. As nearly as I can tell, he hadn't done anything about getting it afloat on the other end, but he was surely waiting for it to arrive. Someday something would happen and everything would be OK. He died waiting.

The old man wasn't the only one who died waiting. A lot of folk have learned to be good waiters. They can't be described as inactive because they do lots of good things as they go through life. Unwittingly, they do good things that aren't directed toward getting them where they want to *be*. Living the good life is somehow supposed to provide magically what they really want. Santa will suddenly arrive on the rooftop with a bag full of "just the right things" if they hang in there long enough.

People who wait for Santa do it in different ways. I know of a lady who has been waiting twenty-three years for her husband to "shape up." Maybe someday he will; up to now, he hasn't shown any indication that he's going to! Some people stay stuck and wait for someone else to make the decisions that will free them. In any event, the theme of waiting for Santa is to expect other people to bring us what we want. Miles Standish, wanting to marry Priscilla Mullens, sent John Alden to ask her in his stead. What he accomplished was to be invited to John and Pris's wedding. Or maybe he's still waiting for her answer.

I just heard of an agency supervisor who spent an evening visiting one of her departments for the first time. She complained the next day that she had felt very uncomfortable during the visit; no one had introduced her to others! She'd spent the whole evening feeling bad while waiting for someone to do something she could have done for herself. Santa didn't come!

This style of behavior is called passivity. We probably learn it in the high chair. We scream and people run for the bottle warmer. We yell and our diapers get changed. Later we learn that the same operation works after we've learned to talk. Make some kind of noise and other people will translate it and do what we want. Archie Bunker shouts, "I'm thirsty," and

Edith fetches his favorite brew. He doesn't have to ask for what he wants. She is supposed to know that's what he wants and to act accordingly. She does, so it works.

The first step of passivity is doing nothing.* When the teacher asks if anyone has a question, half the people will wait for someone else in the group to come up with an interesting one. If no one does, it is a boring class. Sometimes I think that if a fire started in the living room during a cocktail party, three-fourths of the group would wait for someone else to put it out or call the fire department. "Well, I didn't want to be pushy; it was *their* phone." Some folk, when wanting a hug or a conversation, will sit and look wimpy, waiting for someone else (Santa) to pick up the cue and move. When our first efforts don't work, we can escalate the action a tad. If they aren't seeing our wimpy looks, then adding a big, long sigh sometimes helps them *hear* our disires! If the sigh doesn't work, doing a flop on the couch is more obvious because it can be *seen*. With a little patience (and God knows the Professional Waiter has patience) sooner or later someone will ask, "What's wrong?"

When doing nothing fails, the next step is to make a major escalation into what transactional analysts call Over-Adaptation. This means doing something we think the other guy wants us to do. Usually we will employ our favorite Driver—we will Hurry Up, Try Hard, or Be Pleasing or Perfect or Strong. Let's say dad isn't getting the attention he wants and Doing Nothing hasn't improved the situation. He escalates into his Be Strong pattern by doing something very uncomfortable without complaining. Mom takes the hint and comes running with a beer and a back rub which she forces on him along with her usual sermon advising him to slow down and not try to be so strong! Passivity works again.

When our usual way of operating fails us, we can escalate

*J. Schiff and A. Schiff, "Passivity," *TA Journal,* vol. 1:1, p. 71.

into what is termed *agitation,* which is a way of draining energy away from the problem to be solved. You've done that. Remember the last time you were really angry and decided not to deal with it? Instead, you scrubbed the hell out of your car or stove! The anger dissipated as you put energy into your sponge. The problem remained, though. Agitation is behavior that fails to solve a problem. We show our agitation in many small ways, like lighting up a cigarette we don't want, pacing the floor, pounding our fists, tapping our fingers on the table, or, as an indirect consequence, having a muscle spasm beneath one of our eyes. This agitation is usually called Stewing. In some sections it is called Worrying. It is something to do while we wait for Santa to solve the problem. I've seen some Master Stewers in my day. They have trouble understanding that they are really Doing Nothing while waiting. How can that be when they are so busy? Up, down, back and forth, round and round, go through the chain of events one more time, get suggestions, explain what's wrong with all the suggestions, get back up. Nothing? Yep. They're literally working themselves into inactivity.

If agitation fails us, our final resorts are either violence or incapacitating ourselves! Some people throw things, or sometimes their fists. Others drink themselves senseless or have a massive nervous breakdown or such. Most of us will recycle the first three steps until something *does* work. Eventually, time and tide produce success.

Passivity is most often based on our conviction that we can't do what we want done, and it reinforces that conviction.

I've always hated the pastoral prayer in church services. While posing as reverent, intimate conversations with God, they are most often second chances for the pastor to zap the congregation in case it missed his message during the sermon. "Oh, Lord, thou knowest we aren't giving as much to thee and thy work as we ought." (Everyone knows he's looking for babysitters in the crib room.) Some pastors use the pastoral prayer to tell God everything he ought to be aware of, in case he missed his morning paper. "We are thinking this morning of sister Emma Lou and her new baby." If God is what the preacher says he is, he certainly knew about the baby before the preacher did! And presumably before the mother.

I attended a prayer service for preachers. The first guy prayed for twelve long minutes. I counted! When he was through, he had said everything he could possibly think of to pray for. The next guy tried to fake a new prayer, and sounded as if he were struggling. I was seventh in line, so I mumbled something quick about my agreeing with everyone else. I never went back.

The main reason I dislike pastoral prayers is not because they are so boring, but because they discourage people from staying in contact with their own God. Pastoral prayers and those official prayers at banquets and football games are our main contact with "good praying." Since the clergyperson is expected to be a professional "pray-er," the temptation is almost irresistible for him to demonstrate his talents along these lines. Consequently, a "good prayer" is long, covers a lot of subjects, and contains only the best grammar and vocabulary. At the rodeo last week the invocator said, "We sure are real glad to have this little talk with thee." I snickered at the strange blend of Elizabethan English and east Texas country talk. Since most of us aren't too up on good prayer techniques, we say to heck with it and hire out our praying.

One of my best communications with the eternal came when I first saw the Grand Canyon. I had discounted it in advance as being merely a big ditch. I'd seen pictures and wasn't all that impressed. Then I saw *it* and the words popped out: "Awwww, Wow!" That's a prayer, friend. (Another good prayer I've heard of: One of the cardinals in my Private Church was honored by being invited to give the invocation at a football game. According to the story, he stepped to the microphone as fifty thousand heads bent piously and said, "Dear God, you know we're not here to pray. Amen." What a great prayer; but they never invited him back.)

Many prayers encourage passivity by advising people to dump the job on the biggest Someone Else they can think of. A social motto supports that: "God will take care of you." You just tell him about the problem and that heavenly bellhop will do it for you. Want a better job? Tell God and see what he can do; he has some pretty good contacts. If nothing comes of it, you can stay where you are and always say that God didn't *want* you to have a better job. Some people really believe in "letting God do it." Carlyle Marney, the founder of Interpreter's House, once again rearranged my thoughts when he said he hadn't prayed for civil rights for thirty-one years. He quit praying for them when it occurred to him that Christians made up over 51 percent of the population of the country. They could quit praying and do something about civil rights whenever they wanted. In other words, why bother God with something you're in control of?

A few people get so far into "letting God do it" that they refuse to let very sick children get medical assistance, relying instead on their prayers. I figure God already answered their prayers when he sent the medicine! To blame the child's death on God's will is demonic beyond belief.

There is another problem about waiting that I haven't mentioned yet. Frequently we wait for something we don't want in the first place or don't want after we get it. If you waited thirty-eight years to find that out. . . .

Everything does *not* come to people just because they wait. Oh, maybe it would if you lived to be 2,359 years old. No, not even then. Some things are *never* going to come, such as the Fairy Godmother. She came for Cinderella, but no one I know has seen her. Utopia, peace on Earth, an error-free day, or everyone's approval, will most probably never come. Most other things won't come if all we do is wait.

There is something about us that expects the Truly Fine Things in Life to come exploding into our hearts and our days like streaks of lightning, ablaze with neon signs proclaiming them unmistakably for what they are. Not so! My hunch is that even Jesus looked pretty much like the next carpenter. So with the Good Life we're looking for. It probably spends far more time on quiet back streets than it does on the busy boulevards. If we wait patiently for the good things to come to us, not at all prepared to "put it together" for ourselves with what we have, we will experience the sadness of having just barely missed something very good. There is a ring of pathos in the title of the song from *South Pacific,* "This Nearly Was Mine."

We can wait with a telescope stuck in one eye, looking way out yonder for what we want, and miss it passing by in the present time. A nearsighted girl didn't want her boyfriend to know she was myopic. Before he came to visit, she stuck a pin in the bark of an oak fifty yards from her back porch. While sitting on the porch with him, she remarked, "Isn't that a pin over there in that tree?" When her friend admitted he couldn't see anything, she suggested they walk over and take a look. On the way, she tripped over a cow.

We miss a lot when we focus only on what we await. I think one of life's deadliest temptations is to delay action until our "ship comes in." When I was a troop chaplain with the air force, I saw many of the men I worked with putting themselves "on hold" until they got out of the military. They were "doing their time," as if they were in prison. Sometimes we do find ourselves in exile—living for a time in some land or culture or style or situation not to our liking. It is clear to us that we are just passing through, so why bother planting roses? When I left basic training for my first assignment, we were told we would be going overseas within a few months. "Don't unpack," it was suggested. Taking it all pretty seriously, I stayed emotionally packed for about sixteen months before I wised up and settled in. Good thing. I stayed at that base in north Texas for fifty-two months!

Webster's second definition of *waiting* is "in readiness for action." Don't pray for rain unless you have an umbrella somewhere in the vicinity. Healthy waiting looks different from the passive waiting of Losers. An officer I served with in Turkey knew how to wait well. We were there for a twelve-month assignment without our families. The favorite off-duty conversation frequently centered around the general topic of "Oh, my God, look what's happened to me." Not so with Joe! His motto for that year: "I'd rather be in Samsun, Turkey, than anyplace on earth." People thought he was up to something. He was. He was into living as if he were going to spend the rest of his life there. Another man proclaims he is planning to live to be a hundred and fifty years old. He will admit there's a possibility he might not make it; but he plans his life—and operates—like a teen-ager with whole worlds to conquer.

Some things come to him who waits; more things come to the person who saves his waiting for the bus station and gets on with his life. So what if you have to move on just as the roses start coming up? There'll be somebody behind you to enjoy them, and that ain't all bad.

9
Fire? What Fire?

IGNORE IT AND IT'LL GO AWAY

As nearly as I can tell, most of us have a vague understanding that if we *ever* "get it right," we will not only live in a Disneyland world, but mentally our *insides* will be shipshape, too. Neat, clean, and tidy.

Remember the picture on the front cover of the Sunday school bulletin? The family is gathered around father, who is wearing a three-piece suit with a cross in the lapel. He matches the kids, whose outfits are incredibly white. Mom looks like a missionary. They're looking at each other adoringly. Dad has a Bible on his lap. I tried to reproduce that little scene once when my kids were three and six. During Advent, I remember. We gave it up as a bad deal after the second try; it didn't work out quite the way the pictures showed. I even had my clergyman's collar on and it didn't work out. While the setting was similar, our insides were churning before we got through. A six-year-old child isn't terribly interested in Advent prayers, it turned out. It's hard to feel pious while yelling, "Will you please put the flippin' cat's tail back where it belongs?"

Despite the endless problems involved, there remains a social conviction that inner serenity is where it's at, as the saying currently goes. If we could only "get it right," we would feel serene, put-together, harmonious, and "cool." We've come by that conviction honestly. Several generations still living were brought up on the motto "Every day in every way I am getting better and better." Or should be. During World War II we were told we could make it through if we would simply "accentuate the positive and eliminate the negative." A preacher sold a hundred jillion books by retranslating the gospel into *The Power of Positive Thinking.* The general idea was simply to *ignore* the negative aspects of life. Instead of getting clutched when the kids beat on the coffee table with their drumsticks, you should have spent time chortling over the fact that they weren't practicing on your Wedgewood platter! Neat, huh? Mr. Peale's ideas were not all that gross, but the general theme made it clear that our *duty* was to be happy, happy, happy. No bad thoughts, no bad feelings.

Pollyanna was a storybook character who had this way of life down pat. Nothing *ever* came along that got *her* strung-out. Her pinafore never became wrinkled. We of the real world rather snicker at Ms. P., but she is one of our "patron saints." At least we envy her a lot. Wouldn't it be nice if *we* could live that way? After all, we've been told that the healthy person is someone who is positive, smiling, polite, and above all happy—a blithe spirit, cheerfully plowing through whatever. To be cheerful is to be OK.

But it seldom works out that way! I write with throes of labor, with pains similar to those I imagine women suffer in giving birth. Why can't I do it easily, as you're supposed to be able to do? The man with pen, ink, and foolscap, calmly proceeding from paragraph to paragraph, pausing from time to time to take his dog for a walk. Yet just mailing a chapter to the publisher is a trauma for me.

I imagine house husbands get the same "what's wrong with

me?" feeling while scrubbing the latest household grunge off the linoleum. From the inside we surely don't resemble the chic lady on TV who manages to stay neat while doing it in a chiffon dress, pantyhose, high heels and a pleasant smile! The TV woman always looks as if she is on friendly terms with the dirt.

One of the kids is practicing bongo on the coffee table! How come I sit here gritting my teeth and glaring (I'm going to yell in about five minutes!) instead of smiling benignly with paternal affection as they do on "Father Knows Best"? How come I face a tooth extraction with less dignity than the people on "Medical Center" deal with terminal diseases?

Do you recall the last time you had a bad case of the yukkhs? When you were loaded with down-and-wish-I-were-out-so-I-could-take-off-the-gloves feelings? Did you like yourself? My observation is that's the time we most generally find it hard to like ourselves. It's the only time I ever *don't* like myself! "Boy, what a Wimp! Shape up! Quit being a gloom spreader; you're raining on everyone's parade. Go crawl in a hole and pull it in after you, Greer!"

We have social mottoes that support this Never Feel Bad attitude. When I was in my first pastorate, the town of Mineral City, Ohio, had a real tragedy. Annabelle Rudolph was on her way to her first day's work as an assistant superintendent in the school system. She and a semi-tractor-trailer tried to use the same piece of highway while going in opposite directions and Annabelle was killed instantly. As I sat with the family during the next shock-filled hours, I listened to a number of folk tell her parents: "Keep your chin up!" I understand they wanted to reach out in sympathy, but what a tacky thing to say! If ever there was a time for chins to droop, that was it. These folk wanted the chins *up*!

How about, "Whistle while you work"? Happy, happy!! (I

hope some people, my dentist for instance, never do that. Funeral directors, symphony conductors and piano tuners might have problems whistling while they work, too.)

Or, "Let a smile be your umbrella"! I'm probably a charter member of the Let's-Hear-It-For-Smiles Association, but I've never heard that phrase without picturing some turkey standing at a bus stop, empty hand held aloft, big smile on his face, and *dripping wet!* Smiles are useful to show people you're friendly or feeling happy. Smiles tend to be contagious in those situations.

But lots of smile are phony. Some used-car salesmen smile and you're supposed to infer that the brakes on the car you just bought won't give out before you get the car home. Some people smile when they're going into surgery, and the smile is supposed to mean bravery. Lots of people smile when they tell of something harmful to them—like being fired from their jobs or getting drunk again or having made someone mad enough to hit them. Transactional analysts call that a "gallows laugh." Since there's nothing funny about getting your neck stretched, the laugh is a sick one. But what the hell, a smile is an umbrella and will protect you from Something. Or Other.

We are almost fanatically convinced that somewhere, somehow, there is a formula for making negative things disappear forever. For example, managers in business want, and expect, to find a new way to tell their people that a merit increase isn't coming without making the employees feel bad! We know we can figure out a way if we just put our minds to it! The closest we've come so far to finding a formula for eliminating evil is encapsulated in the advice: *Ignore it and it'll go away!*

As a skinny kid with a quick mind and a big mouth, I seemed to encounter a lot of hostile kids in traveling to and from school each day. Some kids take offense at being told their mother wears army shoes or whatever. They figure out ways of getting back at loudmouths. The ways they figure out usually hurt. I had an amazing lack of social skills during elementary school days. My "cute remarks" were basically the whole package. I even provoked my drafting teacher into slugging me once and spent a month wondering why God let such hostile people be teachers.

Those days I spent a lot of time running. I always tried to shorten the time I spent between the protection of mom (watching from down the alley) and the first teacher I could get myself near. The main advice I got from the grown-ups was to ignore them (the kids). "They'll leave you alone." That advice might have worked if I had *started out* with it. But after I'd verbally licked the red off some kid's candy, he wasn't likely to ignore *me*. So, belatedly, I tried ignoring them, which meant I didn't run, which meant I got hit more. The next best advice I got was from Uncle Ed, a survivor from the Civilian Conservation Corps. He had a soft heart and probably was tired of watching me get beat up, so he gave me an eight-minute boxing lesson. The main trick was to step on the other guy's foot so he couldn't get away and then pop him one. The first and only time I tried it, I was so busy looking for the kid's foot that my face was a wide-open target! It's just as well that I didn't get the chance to hit him. They had forgotten to teach me to keep my thumb on the outside of the fist. If I had landed a punch, in addition to my normal aches and pains, I would have hurt my thumb badly and probably spent that day trying to write with my left hand.

Ignore it! Sure. Ignore the fact that your wife's coffee tastes like battery acid? Ignore it when your mate ridicules you in public? Ignore the seven thousand-decibel stereo noises? Ignore the peanut butter smeared on the TV picture tube? Ignore the fact that someone put salt in the sugar bowl? How? For how long? Lots of luck!

There is a corollary motto going around for advanced players. "No, Sam, you can't ignore that; what you need to do is just not *think* about it!" How's that for subtle? I've used sexual fantasies to keep my mind off dentists' drills with a modicum of success, but generally, trying not to think of something only insures that I *will* think about it.

The mottoes continue, inviting us to be Losers by pretending that nothing is really happening. How about: "If you can't say something good about a person, don't say anything"? The kid is setting fire to your curtains? Well, if you can't praise him for his ingenuity, just keep your mouth shut! Joe Yukk has been badmouthing everyone in sight for thirty minutes and you want to tell him that he's in serious danger of being a jerk? Well, don't! You shouldn't think such un-good things in the first place. Your mate has burnt the meat seventeen nights in a row? Don't suggest that she's not being careful; that wouldn't be a "nice thing to say." After all, you have to take the bitter with the sweet.

People who have been weaned on the idea that if you can't say something nice . . . *always* must resort to withdrawal when dealing with negative things. They let the problem continue and try to get out before too much splatters onto them.

Another one: "Every cloud has a silver lining." Nonsense! I've been up in the sky, and some clouds have linings that are as black as coal. Particularly at night. The myth that you can find good in everything is a dangerous one to believe. This slogan invites people to ignore the black and look for the silver. Accepting that notion, some people become cloud collectors. Since silver ore must be subjected to fire before pure silver is extracted, stay in hot water and hope the silver will come. This is patently nonsense. I'm for people making good things happen out of bad events. I'm always cheering for the phoenix to rise out of the ashes; sometimes it does, but you don't need the ashes first.

Along the same line is that oldie: "It'll make you a better person." I think for my fiftieth birthday I'm going to give myself permission to pour water on the first person who says that to someone in my presence. "Go ahead and listen to that boring lecture, it'll make you a BP." Some negative events *do* add to our experience in a helpful way, but most of them leave us less well off and no one is a Better Person for that.

Some things you *can* ignore, such as small children, who have very short attention spans. When they scream, "Mommie, I hate you!" mom doesn't have to make a "federal case" out of it. She can assure the child that she is aware of his unhappiness, knowing full well that ten minutes later the kid will be doing something interesting and have forgotten the "hate."

You can ignore sidewalk barkers and other hustlers. "Hey! You in the green hat there. Come here and let me. . . . Hey! You afraid of your wife, huh? C'mere!" A guy tried to get me into an all-girl revue with the phrase, "What's the matta? You just like boys?" I cranked up an effeminate giggle and asked him how he spotted that so quickly. He blanched and immediately turned his attention to other passersby. His insult was designed to get me to cough up five dollars to prove him wrong and therefore was easily ignored. Most insults are attempts to manipulate our behavior and therefore equally easy to ignore. I think the phrase "consider the source" is a put-down of the other person and not helpful. "Consider the purpose" is a lot more helpful.

Your mate hits you a lick that is not so subtle by saying, "You're the messiest person I know." Considering the purpose, you respond: "Do you want me to pick up my clothes?" You put yourself in a better place than you'd be if you started evaluating just exactly *how* messy you are relative to others of your age and sex.

Passing aches and pains are well worth ignoring. The

human body (like any ship) creaks and groans constantly. There is always some part or other that is "crooked." If we pay attention to all the creaks we will feel pretty unhealthy.

(As an aside, it's important to note that we do ignore hundreds of things each day. I just noticed my windows are filthy. Hadn't noticed that before—been ignoring it. The question is not, "How do I ignore things?" but "How do I decide to pay attention to that in the first place?" Many things we "can't ignore" are in fact somehow important to us so we *choose* to pay attention.)

Some negative events are notable but not worth very much of our energy. Frequently, it is *very* useful to overlook the negative implications and invest our energy in the good stuff. A husband who wouldn't dream of getting involved with a real-life Other Woman, chooses to spend thirty minutes a week with the centerfold women in men's magazines. His wife can get uptight about his "filthy habit," or she can feel good in the knowledge that this is as big as his affairs are going to get.

A man who gets a promotion and an increase in pay would be well-advised to pass over the fact that he didn't get the particular assignment he wanted. He can rejoice in his good fortune and anticipate a later reassignment.

I knew a lady once who ruined thirty months of her life by "accentuating the negative and eliminating the positive." Her husband was a high-ranking officer in the air force and received an important assignment to Okinawa. On that tour of duty it was customary for the man to leave ahead of his family and spend about three months looking for off-base housing. Once he had secured a house, his family could start packing. It took another fifteen months to move into on-base housing. These quarters were really comfortable and all the furniture was supplied by Uncle Sugar. They came in three styles: L-shaped, I-shaped and Breezeway. The colonel's family came to the island together and moved immediately into an on-base house. As I said, he had an important post. But this lady chose to spend two and a half years of her life feeling bad. She had been forced to take an L-shaped house and she was certain the breezeway houses had more status! Boy, was she a miserable person to be around. She wouldn't quit talking about her stupid floor plan! People solved that by staying away from her.

Some things you can ignore; some things you can give short shrift. But some things *can't be ignored.* Try ignoring your tongue while it's squeezed in a vice. Or your taxes. "They" won't *let* you ignore them. You can't really ignore war in your neighborhood or getting passed over for an important promotion. It's next to impossible to ignore getting hit in the face (either with a fist or verbally), especially if it is an ongoing, repetitive thing. It's moderately difficult to ignore the announcement that someone likes everyone in the room but you! Ignoring the loss of something important like a marriage or the death of a parent or a child leaving home or a vocation or a home itself or even a family heirloom *just will not work.*

Your Child Ego State will be only six years old so long as you live. It won't be indifferent to "bad things," no matter how many Bible verses are quoted to you or how hard you try or even what your mommie says. That part of you is going to *hurt* when hurtful or harmful things go on around you. The pain will stay until you decide to *deal* with what's happening.

Bad things come to us in two forms, which I think we ought not ignore. The first is Pure Evil—what theologians call The Demonic. These events are so purely bad, so palpably evil, that they seem as if a person has been at work. People have given this person various names—the Devil; Satan; Mephistopheles; Ahriman; Lucifer; Abaddon; Appollyan; Asmodeus; Beelzebub; Belial. We always give names to things that are very real to us, and the demonic *is* real. I don't believe in a real-life Satan, with or without horns and a tail. Nor do I believe in a real *place* called Hell. (Jesus didn't, so why should I?

He talked about the fires of Gehennah, the village garbage dump. The concept of a bad place where bad people went when they died showed up in Christianity centuries after Jesus lived.) But even if the Demonic isn't a person, it surely feels as if there were someone sometimes! How else can you explain having two flat tires, that your pen is leaking, that you are losing a fat commission, and that your kid is coming down with the croup—all on the same day—if someone isn't picking on you *personally*???

The Demonic is real, and sometimes it comes full blast. Cancer comes "out of the blue" and turns a beautiful, healthy person into an eighty-pound vegetable before it kills her. The gentle folk of two nations find themselves bayoneting each other in an all out war and no one really knows why. People with more than enough money insist on making still more money (often without even wanting more money) by renting horrible housing at horrendous prices to folk with no money. *Nobody* wants inflation or pollution, yet we seem helpless to combat them. As a group we cause both of them, and that in itself is "demonic"!

The Demonic frequently comes masquerading as the Good. And that is perhaps a worse satanic plague. Someone referred to it as "wolves in sheeps' clothing." Haven't you wanted to hit at least 80 percent of the folk who did something "for your own good"?

A woman battling near-terminal cancer asked another woman to pray for her. The second woman's response was demonic: "You wouldn't be in this mess if you'd have lived right in the first place." Honest!

One of my favorite early TV serials was "Paladin," a story about a gunslinger who wore black clothes and silver ornaments and hired his gun out for worthy causes. In one show he stopped a group of villagers who were about to lynch an innocent "horse thief." He spent the half-hour teaching them (he thought) that it was really bad form to rush to the hanging tree just because they thought they were right. He taught them by catching the real criminal. They immediately proceeded to hang the new guy! The show ended with Paladin, astride his white horse atop a hill, witnessing the murder and commenting, "God protect us from the things men do in the name of good!" Some of the most "do-good" organizations are seedbeds for rampant evil.

Some folk (and all of us, some of the time) are involved in wiping out evil. I remember having that for a goal once. My understanding now is that the Demonic is here to stay. Sometimes it will not only hang around, but sit on the throne itself! Pure Evil will not go away just because we've chosen to ignore it. The good news of Jesus' gospel was not that evil, and the forces that work against life, could be eliminated forever, but that there is something we can do about them. For starters we can quit being eligible targets. We can also quit using negative power ourselves.

We don't change much by ignoring reality. No matter how much we powder the face and comb the hair, no matter how fine the casket or comfortable the pillow, a corpse still looks dead. Pretending the body is only sleeping prolongs the agony. Throwing old folk into nursing homes so that "they can be with their friends" deprives both the old *and* the young; it doesn't eliminate the aging process. Running elevated freeways over the slum may improve the scenery for the traveler, but it may also produce a higher crime rate which comes with the "ignoring." Sitting around singing hymns about Beulah Land and how we're Glory Bound (while consigning "the infidel" to Hell) doesn't eliminate evil. It helps it on its way.

We weren't designed to be gods who could eliminate evil and the powers of darkness. Darkness comes with the territory. The seven deadly sins (the things that help us die) are going to be around at least as long as we are. They can neither be ignored nor eliminated. They have to be dealt with.

Not all bad things are Pure Evil. Some are toxic or poisonous. These poisonous things/events/people/places are not evil in themselves. Take sulphuric acid. No, *don't* take it with your coffee. It's toxic! It's not evil; people use it every day for good purposes. But it you get it on your skin, or worse yet inside your skin, it will burn you! Toxic!

Toxic things are those that destroy tissue, somehow hinder our growth, or slow us down. Examples: Alcohol is not "bad." Many use it well and helpfully, but for others alcohol has become toxic and damages the brain. Alcohol is toxic when it produces sickness or accidents and the like.

Some things (or people, or places, or ideas, or values) slow us down and keep us from being what we could be. A job could be toxic, for example, it occupies so much time that we are deprived of any other activity, like being with people we love. "You shouldn't admit weakness to others" could be a toxic idea that poisons the possibility of closeness.

Things that annoy us for more than a minute or two are toxic, I think. If I were to have water dripping on my head while I'm trying to write, I would soon be using energy (to ignore the drops) that could otherwise be used for thinking. Same with shoes that pinch, or clothes that irritate, or people who rub us the wrong way. People who rub us the wrong way frequently don't rub *others* the wrong way, even with the same behavior or words. So their words or behaviors aren't "bad" nor are they toxic for others. But they certainly remain so for us. If the relationship is poisonous, we waste time trying to place blame. Whether we're "too sensitive" or they're "too obnoxious" doesn't matter. We need to separate ourselves from the poison.

People really can poison one another. We spread toxicity

when we work a power play on others by using words or behavior to get them to do something they don't want to do. "I'm
going to pout until you take me to the movies." "I'm going to
be angry until you quit working that puzzle and watch TV with
me." Power plays toxify the other person and invite crazy
behavior in response.

Married folk can poison each other. I recall a couple in one
of my parishes who were two of the nastiest people I have
ever met. She out-nastied him three to one. One day he had a
heart attack and died out of spite, I think. I figured Henrietta
would up her nasties by 600 percent now that she was a
widow. Surprise! Without him in her life, she turned almost
magically into a softer, more understanding person. And then
I understood; *he* was the one full of poison, and she was
bouncing off of that toxic atmosphere. Since then, I've seen
the same phenomenon a number of times.

Parents frequently poison their children with toxic expectations and noxious invitations to feel bad about themselves and
life. Kids can squirt venom at their parents, I know. But they
didn't get toxic in a vacuum. Besides, I figure the parents are
bigger, have been to more goat ropings and county fairs, and
are therefore better able to cope.

The bad things in life, whether evil or toxic, hurt and impair
our lives. What can you do about that? There is only one
thing. *Do* something about it. Get rid of it! Put the acid in an
acid-proof container. Turn off the water spigot or move your
chair to drier places. Buy new shoes or go barefoot. Cut down
the time spent with people who "rub you the wrong way."
You don't *have* to eat broccoli!

Some toxic things will go away if you ignore them. Most of
them won't. Toxicity is aggravated when we ignore it. I know
this happens inside me. When I ignore or discount a part of
me that wants some attention, it flips into a "scream mode." If
I ignore the Kid in me who's scared, he pulls harder and yells

louder. If the Mommie in my head doesn't like what I'm doing, the noises come on stronger until I deal with them. I don't have to follow the orders my Kid or my Mommie send out, but I do have to deal with them.

The same is true with other people, toxic ones particularly. People hate to be ignored. Have you ever been to a party where some bore takes over the conversation? One by one listeners' eyelids start drooping, folk start fidgeting, but no one says or does anything so the bore moves into high gear with still more boring stories. "So I said to Emma, didn't I Emma? I said. . . ." Fritz Perls once said something that strikes me as important. "If someone is boring you to death, do him the honor of falling asleep!" You notice what they're doing! "But what if they get mad?" you ask. How in the world will you be worse off (unless the bore is your boss) if he's miffed? At least his anger won't be so boring! With luck, he may go out to the kitchen and drink. Or leave.

Perls isn't my role model, but he did a lot of things that make sense to me. I heard a story concerning his eightieth birthday celebration at some big hotel.* Bigwigs from all over the nation were there. When Fritz entered, they all stood and applauded, and he was really pleased with the warm welcome. Then the master of ceremonies (apparently a stuffy man of unusual insensitivity) began a long, intricate, boring speech "of tribute." On and on and on it went. Halfway through one of his paragraphs, Fritz got up—and *left*. I think that's marvelous. Some "presents" we have a right to refuse!

I think it's important to mention here that Perl's departure was *not* an insult to the speaker—the speaker was insulting Perls with his Rape of Time by being more concerned with his own agenda than he was with his listeners.

Most folk experience a problem when they want to deal

*If this story didn't happen, it should have.

with things that distress them. How do they deal with negative things (or people) in an "OK" way? Having been taught as kids that someone must lose every conflict, we continue to be certain that when there is a "sticky wicket" to go through, someone must be the Loser. Usually, out of kindness or deference or timidity, and frequently out of habit, *we* decide to be the Losers. Perls could have opted for Losing by sitting through the rest of what was to come. He could have laid Loserhood on the speaker by turning to his dinner companion and starting a loud conversation, thereby sharing the speaker's time. The speaker had a right to talk for a long time and to be boring! Those he talked to had a right to listen and be bored, or even interested!

Perls had a right to be bored and to leave. I can only imagine what Perls was thinking, but I've a strong hunch he wasn't saying "That man is a bore," but rather, "I'm bored!" What's the difference? A lot! The first lays Not OKness on the speaker. The second accepts responsibility for not liking what he heard.

When dealing with unacceptable events and people, we have four choices of approach. We can decide to lose or to make the other guy lose. We can decide that there ain't no hope anyway and insure that both sides lose. Or, we can choose the route that provides the optimum chance for both sides to win. That's what Eric Berne and Bob Goulding termed the "I'm OK—You're OK" position of transacting. (Look at Chapter 3, pages 38 and 39 to refresh your memory about how OK-ness looks.)

The speaker in the example above could decide to be a Loser by dwelling on what a horrible thing he had done. He could put Perls in the Loser's position by thinking, "How dare that man insult me by leaving! He should have stayed to avoid embarrassing me. He owed it to us, for after all, we were doing it for *him!*" Or he could deal from the OK-OK position by noting that what he had said (or how and for how *long!*) was not something that jazzed the old man. From that position he is further able to learn something from the event. Next time he might pay more attention to how the guest of honor is reacting and time his words accordingly. He might take Before Dinner Speech Lessons. He might decide to feel honored when asked, but decline further invitations to address crowds, particularly those including Fritz Perls. Otherwise, he could only spend his time defending himself, attacking Perls's Bad Form, or both! We don't learn much while defending or attacking.

When operating from the OK-OK position and wanting both sides to win, we will immediately answer the question, "What's causing the problem?" There are only two answers. Either you are invading me or my air space, or I am reacting poorly. If you are banging on my head or yelling in my ear or breaking the points off my pencils, you are invading my air space. When this happens, I need to take effective action. My first choice is to begin negotiations. "Hey, I don't like you doing that. Will you stop?" If you say no, I can give you information about what effective action I plan to take.

I once refused to let the kids watch TV, since they had refused to do their chores. I had turned the set off, but they jumped up and turned it back on. I didn't want to yell at them or hit them, so I went to my tool rack and returned with a set of wire cutters and snipped the cord! It was my set and I knew how to repair the damage for eighteen cents. They were both square-mouthed with grief. (There is nothing so temporarily worthless as a TV set with no plug!) In the talk-through afterward, we processed what had happened, and we all learned something. I'm convinced that yelling, hitting, or giving in would not have been 10 percent as effective.

Frequently though, the problem lies in my reaction. Once after camping with a group, I decided to stay on when it was time to leave since I had nothing scheduled for the next day.

That night, in a near-empty campground, I enjoyed my aloneness. Then I heard a radio blaring from another camp. Talk about mad! I spent five minutes mumbling things such as, "They should have more respect!" "How could they. . . ." Whatever possessed them to. . . ." I weighed alternatives like storming over there or reporting them to the Management. Then it occurred to me; I could just barely *hear* the radio! I don't know what impelled me to make a mountain out of a wart, but it didn't have anything whatsoever to do with an invasion of my air space. I was reacting in a non-useful way. Understanding that, I could either change my mood or accommodate myself to what was happening.

To do this kind of sorting out from a Win-Win position, we have to feel OK about ourselves. I think there are two sorts of folk. Saint Paul, when writing to some early Christians, referred to Children of Light and Children of Darkness. That usually gets translated into Good Guys and Bad Guys. I prefer to see the distinction another way. I think it refers to how people see themselves and others. Children of Light see themselves as basically OK. Clean plates, if you will. As these people go through life, some dirty spots develop; they say, "Shucks!" and wipe the dirt off. When they do good things, it's as if they polished the china. The plate was already clean, but now it's glistening. When it gets dirty again, well, that happens and the only thing to do is to clean it again.

Children of Darkness don't see themselves as OK or clean. They know, deep in their bowels, that they are dirty through and through and *paper* plates to boot. Not willing to look like Dirty Paper Plates, there's only one thing to do—find some clean new pieces of paper plates and paste them over the dirt. If they're good at jigsaw puzzles they can squeeze the pieces tightly together and start looking like clean plates. They don't *feel* clean, but what the heck.

There are three problems with this approach. One, the glue

doesn't hold sometimes so you have to keep regluing. "Let me tell you for the umpteenth time how I became an eagle scout when I was only fourteen!" Second, other folk sometimes chip away at the "pastie" and that means war! "I came by that piece of clean-platedness honestly. And you can't take it away from me. What do you mean you're done talking about football? If I can't tell you all the statistics I know, my clean-spot will fall off." Again, life keeps dumping food on my clean plate. Dark spots appear (like having someone walk out on your after-dinner speech!) If there's anything psychologically worse than that, I can't imagine it—to *be* a dirty plate with a clean piece glued over it and then getting "dirtied." Children of Darkness *have* to make issues out of *every* spot and stain.

Children of Light go through life with a positive attitude. Life generally is a ball, but sometimes, when things get grim, they are dealt with. One of the jolliest TV half-hours I ever saw was on "This Is Your Life." At the time, the program was long on maudlin events, and Ralph Edwards frequently featured people who had experienced a lot of misery. That particular evening he had a dilly—his guest had really been through the rapids. But each time he recalled some event ("And then a week after you delivered your baby you broke your leg") she would break into gales of laughter. The more misery Ralph produced, the funnier she thought it was. By the end of the show he was really looking nervous! Wasn't working out the way he had thought.

For Children of Darkness, life is always a swim through a sewer. Back in seminary, I left the dorm one morning delighting in the beautiful spring day. Touches of winter were in the air, but the sky was crystal-clear, and dry and glorious. Turning to a classmate, I commented on the wondrous weather. The best reply he could come up with was, "Good time to catch a spring cold!" Bless his heart. If he hasn't changed in the meantime, these past twenty-odd years must have been one horror after another for him. Children of Darkness have to be on the alert for every nuance that might foretell some dirt a'comin'.

Children of Light, people who have accepted their right to be alive and to be human, will ignore those things that can be ignored and deal effectively with those that can't. Children of Darkness will try either to ignore all the "bad stuff that is constantly coming down" and put on a plastic Happy Face, or they will go through life attacking everything that comes down the pike.

I don't think this is necessarily a case of either/or. Picture a continuum—a line with light at one end and dark at the other. Each of us is at some point along that line. I'm suggesting that the closer we locate ourselves to the light end, the happier and more abundant our lives will be.

10

Once More with Feeling

IF AT FIRST YOU DON'T SUCCEED, TRY, TRY AGAIN!

I never was much of a golfer. Despite the fact that it took me so *long* to get around the course, I kept going back to play. There were a lot of good things about playing golf. I got more swings for my dollar than most guys. I pretended golf put me in the same category with the Big Boys. I even got to know some of them. I could talk the jargon and swap the stories at the nineteenth hole, golf's euphemism for saloon. I enjoyed the beauty of the fairways and greens. But on balance, it was a fairly miserable operation for me. All my golf balls had "smiles" sliced into them—those that weren't in the lake, that is, or hiding in some thicket. It must have been worse for other golfers who threw golf bags into lakes and broke putters over their knees.

It was the Great Shot that kept me playing such miserable golf for as long as I did. Every now and then accidentally I would smack a beauty, three hundred yards straight down the fairway! When that happened, I would hitch up my pants the way Arnie Palmer does, smile crookedly, and say to myself, "Now I am back on my game!" That occasional good shot kept me in sand traps and in the rough and out in the woods the other 99 percent of the time. Ninety-nine percent of the time I was mad (or feeling dumb) because I wasn't "on my game."

Take golf lessons? Why would I want to do that? You just saw what I can do! I'm just not getting it all together; I don't need lessons, I just need a little more practice. If only I didn't have to cut the grass on Sundays!"

That self-deception, so familiar to many of us, is like insisting on wearing a watch that won't work on the basis that it *does* show the correct time twice a day). Psychologists have shown that random reinforcement (being rewarded unexpectedly) is the strongest kind of motivation. That unexpected good shot reinforced my intention to play golf. The hands on the watch were just correct once more, so why throw away the watch?

While studying random reinforcement, behavioral scientists used a "Skinner Box." This is a device into which pigeons are placed. The pigeon is supposed to peck at a particular button, and when he gets the right one, some food drops out. He soon learns which is the food button and which is not. In their experiment, however, the scientists discovered that the pigeons associated more than one thing with getting the food. If the pigeon inadvertently lifted his right foot at the same time that he pecked at the button, he would thenceforth repeat both the pecking and the one-legged pigeon routine. We, too, tend toward similar clumps of behavior, performing ineffective maneuvers that we suspect will help get the job done.

I have a framed sign on my office wall, reading:

> "!yaw siht
> ti enod
> syawla evah
> ew tuB"

(For those of you too tired to translate, it says, "But we have always done it this way!") We do things the way we have *always* done them until we find another, simpler way to do them—and then only if we are confident that we will be equally as safe, or well-off. As I have indicated earlier, many of the things we do are somehow connected with survival issues. We once learned to survive by doing things that way, and we are most reluctant to change for fear of *not* surviving.

When I was a kid, we moved to a house about three blocks from my mother's sister. Her son was my age and I wanted to go play with him. Being only eight, I was given some really simple directions to get there, but they involved going three blocks out of my way. I went *twice* the distance, *but I knew where I was!* After a half-dozen visits from me, my aunt discovered my route and tried to show me the quicker, easier way. Huh-uh! I wasn't *about* to get lost in a strange city for the sake of saving some steps! She was smart enough to suggest that my cousin could hold my hand and show me the way. I figured that if we got lost we could at least do it together, so I consented. Three blocks later, I was ablaze with glee at my discovery of a shorter route; from then on you couldn't have forced me to go the long way.

A lot of the things we do fall into that category, especially the *ineffective* things we do. Like yelling. Sometimes yelling is really effective, like screaming *"Duck"* when a baseball is headed straight at someone's head. (It's effective unless he starts looking around for a mallard.) Most of the time, yelling fails to get much done. Some parents yell at their children in imitation of the Viking Lady in an opera—the one who wears a minnow bucket bra, carries a spear, and screams at the audience for an hour or so. They suppose the kids are moving *because* they have yelled at them. I think people move *despite* the yelling. In any event, on a scale of one hundred, yelling produces about a "two." But everyone else yells and sometimes it seems to work, so we keep it up. "Practice makes perfect"!

Sometimes parents of teen-agers stay stuck with the process

of "managing the kids." It worked when they were little, so why shouldn't it now when they are thirteen and fourteen? If they are disturbed when I lay out their clothes and plan their weekends, it means they are ungrateful. "Someday they'll thank me!" (How is that for a Slogan For Misery?)

Lots of people work to get ahead and fail to notice that they never do. They blame it on fate, or poor potty training, the times, or the Democrats, and work harder. If you look around you will notice a lot of organizations that crank up massive efforts but obtain precious few results. Business conference meetings, church committee meetings, and scads of community organizations manufacture prodigious "Minutes of the meeting of. . . ." reporting accomplishments which would also have resulted from a three-minute phone call. How come? Well, they've always done it that way!

If there is one thing we respect, it's effort. "Give him an 'E' for Effort, gang!" So what if he failed; he tried, and that's what counts, isn't it?" *Trying.* Our frontier days from Plymouth Rock to Oregon have turned us into a nation of Grunters. We respect results, but we *really* are turned on by Grunting.

I've heard it doesn't matter who wins or loses a football game; what matters is how the game was played. If that's so, why do they always keep score?

I recall an officer in the military who spent a year on a base running about in a great flurry of activity. At the end of the year he had done very little. His replacement accomplished far more in a month than the first man had all year; but when he wasn't actually doing something, he would stroll about and do a lot of what is called visiting. After two months of this, the adjutant called him in and told him he was getting a bad name among the other officers for not carrying his share of the load. The adjutant suggested that he get with the program "as his predecessor had." We reward Grunting.

Grunting isn't bad; I'm suggesting that it has no value apart from the results it produces. I picture a man driving a nail with a little bitty hammer. He grunts; he sweats; he swears mightily—but the twelve-penny nail just stares back at him. His grunting is for naught. He needs a bigger hammer.

The Protestant Work Ethic (the name theologians and others have given to our insistence that "work" is always good and "no-work" is always bad) tells us that Bearing Down is the solution to everything. Bear down on the lever. Bear down on your math problems, your marriage, your job. This made a lot of sense in the frontier days when we really needed a lot of Grunting just to stay alive. With the woods full of Indians and wild animals, and with the woods only six feet from the front door, *somebody* had to grunt with the axes, hammers, and shovels. It took grunts to build roads and wells and houses and farms. The community simply couldn't afford to have minstrels and wastrels lying about "having a good time." We had to get on with it.

So we learned to respect Grunting. I think Bearing Down is still good for women in labor, for people trying to shut suitcases that are too full, and for pushing marshmallows into a coke bottle. It is useful for pulling out nails, carrying wheelbarrows full of dirt, and trying to win a marathon race.

Bearing Down is *not* useful for thinking, sex, living together, golf, and most other situations. No sensible person would decide that if taking two aspirins is good, thirty aspirins would be fantastic. Yet in daily life we constantly worship at the altar of "the same thing only more." "Once more with feeling!"

When confronted with the inability to repair a relationship of ours by explanation, we resort to *more* explanation. If we talk too much and people walk away, we try to get them back by talking *more*. If thinking something through doesn't work, we try to think *harder*. It's as if we never get over the old high school cheer, "Hit, 'em again, hit 'em again, harder, harder!"

Bearing Down is not useful in finding Salvation, or The

Abundant Life, or Mental Health—or whatever it is you call what we're all looking for. Yet we insist it is. "Oh, you still aren't happy? You need to have more faith." "You need to get your doctrines more accurate (and please come to me for the corrections)." "You need to pray more." "You need to get out more." "You need to read more." In each case, we insist that it isn't the *method* that is wrong, but the *amount*. A little more will do you. But it seldom does.

We stay with our method because society rewards us for doing so. *"If at first you don't succeed, try, try again!"* The granddaddy of mottoes for success! Are there many children who have not heard the tender story of *The Little Engine That Could?* How the little engine chugged with great pain up the steep mountain saying words to the effect that, "Oh Golly. This is what you call one helluva impossibility." But then the gods of locomotion finally got him thinking positively. Pretty soon he was saying, "I think I can, I think I can." (Kids love this part, because it *sounds* like a locomotive talking.) And with still more time he was saying, "I know I can, I know I can." And finally he *did* make it to the top of the mountain. Great story. But I wish I had a dollar for *every* person I know who is Grunting her way up some stupid mountain she doesn't want to be on top of in the first place. Grunters never stop at the top to enjoy the view; they build another mountain that they can Grunt up!

A classic example of a Grunter is a man I'll call Alfred Whipnoodle. Fred was one of the crew aboard the Skookum III, a stays'l schooner on which a colleague and I were conducting a management development seminar. We were teaching executives to sail and processing how they dealt with stress, with new experiences, and with working with other people. Using this data, we could translate a lot of information into their "back home at work" experiences. Fred was a Grunter, we quickly discovered. He got results but they often were so enveloped by his grunts as to be invisible. He even got seasick, which provides a lot of grunting all by itself. He wouldn't give up and take care of himself, though.

One night while beating out of a channel in the teeth of a blue-norther, old Fred was up in the bows, pulling on a line and barfing, alternately. Even telling him we didn't need him didn't help; he flatly wouldn't quit. At night he would sleep at the top of the companionway, and everyone coming up on watch would step on him. He'd grunt and go back to sleep, waiting for the next guy to step on him. Seventy-three feet of boat and he picked the *one* place where he couldn't possibly get a good night's rest. (The happy ending to this story is that Fred did get in touch with what he was doing and realized he was doing the same thing with the rest of his life. He went home and made a lot of changes in a big hurry. Last I heard, he was more productive than before and a lot happier.)

In Chapter 3 I wrote about the Drivers that impel us to actions we think will put us in a better place—Be Perfect, Please Me, Hurry Up, Try Hard, and Be Strong. I showed you how they frequently bring misery instead of the goodies we expect. Yet each of these is held in reverence by society at large. We assume these are "good ways to go," regardless of whether or not they are effective. "If at first you don't succeed. . . ." Be more perfect, please more people, go faster, bear down more, carry more. The Driver pattern is clearly OK; we need to "try, try again!"

Our patterns of ineffective efforts are further supported by what Eric Berne called "discounts." A discount takes place when our Conceptual Grid distorts reality by seeing only a portion of it. When a store discounts an item, it knocks off part of the price and pretends it isn't there. There was a time when everyone thought the world to be limited to the "flat" area within eyesight, thereby discounting the earth by about 89 percent. Because of our inexperience and lack of information, we "knew" the world was flat. With that distortion we refused to explore any further and limited our own world.

A study by social psychologists discovered that over 25 percent of normal social conversation involves discounts. My hunch is that we discount at least that much with our Conceptual Grids—the ways we look at our world. Our patterns for dealing with the world are greatly affected by these distortions. Each discount deprives us of a part of our world. I don't have to insist that Africa doesn't exist to avoid going there. I know it's there; I choose not to go. Since I admit it exists, I can go there if I want to! Or not go. A discount gives me no choice.

We can discount other people and do—a lot! "He's too dumb to understand." (He has an IQ of 137 but a nasty habit of disagreeing with people.) "What do you expect of a woman?" (Females are supposed somehow to be lacking in something.) "If I told him, it would destroy him." (Words affect his cellular structure just as hydrocloric-acid would.) "She doesn't know what she wants." (But we do; her brain put the wrong address on the message and we have it.) "You never listen to me." (She heard you, Charley; she's just not following your instructions.)

Want some more? "You don't know what's good for you." (You missed school the week the teacher explained to the rest of us what is good for *you*.) "You shouldn't do that." (God just sent me a new set of Stone Tablets; try and stop me from explaining what I think they said.) "Green doesn't go with blue." (What in blazes does *go* mean? Oh, you mean it *clashes*? To whom?) "You always yell." (Meaning "more than I want to listen to.")

Children get discounted a lot, and many family battles originate from the seeds of those discounts. "Put on your sweater; it's cold!" (Meaning, "Are you ever stupid, Kid! You don't even know when you're cold!") "Go to bed; you're tired." (Same translation).

Children need guidance! I hasten to add that they cease being children (in reality, if not in parents' minds) when they pass through puberty, about the time the hair and the hormones start realigning themselves. After that they don't need guidance any more than other grown-ups. Like the rest of us they could probably use some, and will, but only when they choose to. Same as with Grown-Ups.

Prior to puberty, they undoubtedly need "raising." There's a kicker involved, though. As children pass through the various stages of development, they need different *kinds* of guidance! The problem is that just as we start getting the hang of good parenting for the early stages, the kid graduates. What now? Frequently we decide to keep on doing what we did. For example, a three-year-old still needs a shepherd to keep him out of the traffic. His mind hasn't connected traffic with danger. By age five that connection is easily made if the child is allowed to experience safely how that works. To scream at a ten-year-old, "You're standing too near the street" discounts the fact that she can figure out for herself what "too near" is. (Is he *really* mentally defective? Or are we expressing our reluctance for him to act on his own, apart from us?)

Expressing your dislike of blue jeans is a factual statement. Saying however gently, "Would you please take off that impossible outfit?" discounts the right of the person wearing them to clothe herself. It also discounts taste which is obviously different; but different doesn't mean wrong.

(I'm not advocating what is currently called permissiveness. Saying "do whatever you want, I could care less" is not permissive; I think it is callous and conveys the additional message that the offspring is unloved. Kids who are in trouble because they were allowed to do whatever they wanted are not hurting from too much freedom; usually they are certain in their guts that no one really cares.)

Such discounts invariably produce the response (spoken or

un-), "Honestly, mother, you treat me like a child!" Sure! That's exactly what is going on. When *any* of us is discounted, we react with some intensity. Families fight a lot because par ents insist on discounting their offspring, and kids discount their parents. Discounting is deadly.

I started to name this book *Not in Front of the Kids* for several reasons, but American editors, as C. S. Forrester pointed out, "always want to change the title." A very socially approved discount of kids is Protecting Them From Something. Some parents will not fight in front of the kids, as if the knowledge that mom and dad are people who also fight like other people will somehow cause irreparable damage. No one has ever fooled a kid into thinking that mom and dad never fight. They get awakened at 3 A.M. and know what the shouting means. They wonder why it's so hush-hush during the daytime. Something terrible must be going on.

If a kid is over six, he or she is old enough to understand fights. I'm in favor of parents telling their children, and certainly teen-agers, that they are about to have a donnybrook, that they don't intend to hurt each other, and that they most probably will not break up the family. (If the latter is a possibility, I think the kid could use some fair warning.)

Young people from birth to twenty are invariably three to ten years ahead of where most folk see them. Discounting their factual talents and capabilities can only lead to trouble; if not immediately, then down the line. Ever see a parent cutting the meat on his twelve-year-old's plate? Usually that is not an act of kindness but a discount. ("Well, it's so tough for her!") Fifteen years later he's still doing it by paying her car insurance, or such, and wondering why she's "a little irresponsible." She never had much of a chance to *be* responsible; they told her she should be, but then they went ahead and took over her responsibilities for her.

Little is accomplished by keeping young people away from

funerals in order to protect them from the trauma of death. "Grandma's gone bye-bye" to a six-year-old is confusing, especially when she has already buried two sparrows and a cat when no one was looking!

Sometimes I forget how advanced kids are and discount them to my disadvantage. One day the kids and I were visiting my wife, Barbara, after major surgery. It was the third day afterward and she was feeling poorly, to understate it. Each time she was demonstrably sick, Dan and Julie would look upset and give me "let's get out of here" looks. I interpreted that to mean "we don't like unpleasant things," and a part of me really did an angry about that! When we left I was still hot under the collar. I saved my speech until I had cooled a tad, letting them know I was angry by screeching the wheels and staying grimly silent. After we had eaten, I began one of my better organized Sermons for Young People (number thirty-seven). It was a fine speech about having to "take the bitter with the sweet" and "loving means caring." You may recognize the pattern.

The main message of "Did You Ever Mess Up!" was so strong that I was amazed to see them (seventeen and fourteen at the time) listening with interest instead of contrition. During an appropriate break in the sermon, Dan spoke for the two of them. "Would you like to know what was going on with us, Dad?" What could I say? He explained they were no strangers to Throwing Up, having seen it often, sometimes serving on the clean-up crew for sick friends. They recalled how embarrassed they felt when they were sick in someone else's presence. "We thought mom would be a little more comfortable if she didn't have an audience, so we really wanted to get going." What I had taken for uncaring actions were in reality a different form of "we care very much." Before they had finished talking, I was already using an imaginary eraser to make my sermon go away from the imaginary blackboard in front of us! I had arrived at an incorrect conclusion by discounting their love for their mother. Happily, they didn't decide to feel bad just because I wanted to preach.

Not only can we discount others but we can also discount ourselves by seeing ourselves in unreal ways. "I'm too scared/busy/angry to do what I might otherwise do." "I'm not clever enough to think up different ideas." "I'm not good enough to be liked." "I don't know where to turn." "I have to (do something)." Using the last example, let me illustrate the discount. The only thing we *have* to do is die. I cannot think of another "have to." Every other "have to" is in fact a "choose to." I don't have to eat; I choose to eat rather than face the alternatives. Same with going to work or to school or cooking dinner. What about taxes? I don't have to pay them; I can make them come get it (since they're collectors) and pay the penalty for being late, or I can refuse to pay and go to prison. I choose to pay up!

"So what?" you say. "It's only a matter of semantics!" Sure, it's a matter of words, and that isn't so "only"! Words are one of the major tools we use in programming our heads. Consequently, the ones we choose to employ can be important supporters of our ineffective behavior patterns. Each time we discount ourselves by saying "I have to" or "I can't" (when we could if we chose to) we leave ourselves feeling unnecessarily victimized and impotent. We will feel victimized by powers beyond our control and powerless to do what needs doing. The world isn't victimizing us; our *words* are. Every discount involves a choice of words that distorts reality and leads us down the road to a one-down position.

On the other side of the coin, we frequently give words *more* power than they have. This can keep our ineffective patterns of behavior going, too. Early in life we learned that words have some strange results when spoken aloud. People fainted and blanched at the sound of some of them. People would do "hurt feelings" when certain phrases were spoken Some words were "dirty," like $%¢&% and @#*¢&. We didn't understand *how* that was, but people let us know that *words are magic!* Ever hear a parent urge a child to "say the magic word, *please*"? We *teach* our kids that some words are magic. No wonder we say later in life "But he called me a (name) " The word got said, so now something has to happen as a consequence.

We come by this understanding honestly. In early Bible days the Hebrews believed that words were *things*. Do you remember the story of Isaac, old, blind and feeble, who wanted to give his blessing to his twin sons? His plan was to give his primary blessing to Esau, the hairy, out-of-doors and athletic boy who was the firstborn of the twins. Isaac's wife, Rebekah, preferred Jacob, the secondborn. He was an unhairy, indoors, cerebral type of boy. So she worked a trick. She put Jacob into some skins that made him feel like Esau and trotted him in for the blessing that was to be Esau's. Jacob was fooled until after the blessing and had to make up a second-rate one to give to poor Esau. Why didn't he simply "erase" the one he gave to Jacob, and do it over again for the hapless Esau? He couldn't, given their understanding that words were real things. He had already fired the bullets and they had landed; the only thing left to do was to fire some different bullets!

The name of God was the biggest word/thing of all. It was such a biggie that when they read it on paper they would *say* another name that was made up just for such occasions. To speak the real name was considered blasphemy. That belief is still with us. I read in the paper this past year of some unfortunate man who has spent three years in a state prison for "blasphemy." He swore at the wrong time. Magic.

It is usually our *methods* and not our efforts that lead us into "bad places." As we continue believing our discounts and using inaccurate words to program our actions, we condemn ourselves to doing things the same old way, effective or not. Given that, we can only "try, try again."

There is a good side to the motto. It has helped teach us perseverance and determination, both good qualities. It has probably eliminated a lot of halfway, so-so efforts doomed to failure by their very faintheartedness. It counteracts the tendency to say, "If at first you don't succeed, to hell with it!" But as I've shown, perseverance and determination are worthless if the *method* is wrong.

What about Failing To Accomplish? In our society it is almost the Worst Possible Sin, so we urge each other to "try, try again." I would like to change the motto. "If at first you don't succeed, give it one more healthy go; if you still fail, stop and think it over."You're on the brink of a marvelous learning opportunity. Sometimes a moment's reflection makes it obvious that still more effort is needed. Three more blows will do it. A longer lever is needed to get more leverage.

More frequently, I suspect, another method is called for— another path to get to our goal. Have you ever tried to take a cover off something and it resisted your efforts? So you gave it a good healthy "try again" and discovered that two little screws were still doing their job, only now the plastic is all broken and you have to head for the white glue.

Meeting resistance does not always mean failure. Frequently, it means you have to take yet another path before pulling hard. We've all had the experience of trying to pull off a screw-on lid, or unscrew a pull-off one. The same is true of many other operations. Trying to coax someone to move who isn't going to do so unless forced won't work. Trying to force someone who simply needs coaxing won't work. Trying to remain silent around someone who wants an explanation for something won't work. Trying to explain to someone who won't listen won't work.

"If at first you don't succeed. . . ." It may be a sign worth paying attention to. I am learning to pay attention to what I call Closed Doors. Whenever a door I want to walk through closes in front of me, I immediately suspect (unless I fall into some old patterns of frustration) that something useful to me might be going on. As I look back over past experiences, I realize that I have never had a door close in front of me without another door opening up. Perhaps it was open all along. The Second Doors led to even finer events than I had hoped for with the first. I have also spent a lot of time knocking my head "jiggly," banging stubbornly against a firmly closed door. Sometimes I succeeded in crashing my way through and discovered that I didn't like what I found. Sometimes my "failure" was in fact my way of sabotaging my own efforts, knowing it wouldn't be all that good.

Fighting to get our own agenda accomplished shows perseverance and determination, and it isn't always worth it. When the man from Nazareth sent his disciples out for the first time, he told them that if people weren't turned on by what they had to say he wanted them to move on to the next town. Shake the dust off their sandals and get on with it. Somewhere else there were people who would be eager to hear what they had to say. We have X amount of energy at our disposal each day. The energy we use banging our heads against a brick wall cannot be used in other ways. Remember the tests in school? If a really hard question appeared early in the test, I would think, and grunt, and make a dozen passes at answering it. And then I would try thinking some more. Two such questions could fill the whole period successfully, leaving me with fourteen other questions unanswered. I could have answered them if I'd given myself the chance! I'm grateful to the person who taught me to answer the easiest questions first and save the hardest ones for last. My grades went up.

Sometimes reflecting on failure *before* we begin the head-banging reveals that we need to abandon the task for a while.

And is *that* a bitter pill for success-oriented people to swallow! Give up the ship? Abandon the program without giving it your all? Never! Every now and then, giving up is *precisely* the right path, not to failure but to success. Often the time isn't right for what we propose to do. People who won't listen to us today may well listen eagerly tomorrow. Things people don't know what to do with today become very useful in a week or so. Yesterday's leftovers become today's banquet "when the time is right."

Knowing whether to produce more effort or choose another path or give it up for now makes a lot of difference.

My own personal preference is to look for options. *If at first you don't succeed, try something different.* If what I am doing isn't working the first time, it most probably won't work the second time. I need another way to go. I can call on my own creativity and that of others to find more options.

Our creativity is one of our finest talents—and we all have some. When you were four years old you were a super-creative, superimaginative little person. You had a hundred ways to skin any cat that came along. Unfortunately, most of that capability was trained out of us by the various societies around us. Sally Frumphumper goes bouncing off to school with many talents. She soon finds out that they don't count for much. In her first class, the teacher explains that for exercise, the class is going to skip around the room. Sally is so excited! In the past four months she has learned seven new and different ways of skipping. Which one to use—the twice on one foot, once on the other routine or the "holding your foot to the outside" number? Which one? She tries a couple of them, only to be told each time that she is getting it wrong. *"This* is how we skip," explains the teacher, who really wants the girl to get it right for her own good. *

---

*Liladee Bellinger, a transactional analyst who specializes in helping people realize their childlike talents, gave me this analogy.

Same thing in art class. When the teacher tells them she is going to let them draw pictures, Sally immediately remembers thirty-seven pictures she's been wanting to draw. One will show people how God looks! And there's a checkered zebra in light blue she has been wanting to do, and a three-legged man with his hair on upside down, and a. . . . "We're going to draw a flower," says the teacher. "Neat," thinks Sally. She's got a green rose with orange leaves and soft, mushy thorns she has been saving for just such an occasion. By the end of the class it has been made clear to her that the rose will be red with green leaves, and that she hadn't stayed inside the lines where she belonged. So much for creativity.

We don't give up our creative urge all at once, nor over one such event. Over and over we are told that our "bright ideas" are wrong. Many of us finally decide one day that being imaginative isn't all that worthwhile. "There isn't a five-legged frog under your bed, young man. No ice cream for you tonight until you learn to quit imagining things."

"Quit imagining things!" "Oh, you're just imagining things (like a dumbbell)." Imagining things is *wrong*! So we give it up for life. "I can't imagine what he's thinking." "I can't imagine another way to do something." That's why books and magazines on interior decorating are so popular. We *hire* our imaginations. Inventors are people who imagined something different and then imagined how to get it done. Creative designers are people who imagine new designs. Architects imagine new building shapes and materials.

If Trying Hard isn't working, we can "imagine" a new image. You can do something different if you decide not to scold yourself or be embarrassed if it isn't perfect the first time.

Imagine that.

11

Up the Creek with *a Paddle*

*BLESSED ARE THE MEEK,
FOR THEY SHALL
INHERIT THE EARTH*

Harry Truman is alleged to have reported a conversation he had with Winston Churchill. The prime minister of England had been bad-mouthing his rival, Clement Atlee, and Truman felt the need to say a more positive word about the man. He mentioned that he had always admired Atlee's modesty. "Well!" retorted Churchill, "he has so much to be modest about!"

While Atlee's behavior may have bothered Winnie, millions of others would see him as "getting it right." To say that he is living a modest life is not a put-down in our society, but an encomium. Even the second Beatitude declares that the meek will be blessed and inherit the world. So if you want to conquer worlds, be meek! As commonly understood today, *meek* means to be weak and ineffective, quiet and mousy. It even rhymes with squeak. It means mild, spiritless, inoffensive, and above all *little*. The two words are used together as in the phrase, "He was a meek little man." Now who in the pluperfect hell ever wanted to live a life resembling those words?

Yet that seems to be the goal. Apparently, God loves a

Loser. After all, one of the great Christian happenings was when his son let people crucify him. Sweet Jesus, meek and mild. (I've always wondered if, had Jesus been killed in Texas, we would wear fourteen-carat gold, jewel-encrusted *electric chairs* on little chains about our necks?)

The fact that we have turned submissive meekness into an art form is illustrated by the current wave of workshops and classes on "assertiveness." We *know* we are not assertive. "Why didn't I tell the salesperson I didn't want the cup with the chip in it?" "Well, I didn't want to have her think . . . so I decided I'd just go ahead and pay it anyway." "But it was the boss's *wife* who kept spilling her drink on me." "I thought I should wait until someone offered it to me." "I'll take the little one, thank you." "Well, she asked me to so I had to go along with her." Squeak.

Anti-assertiveness is mammothly supported by our society, no matter what we say. Don Merrideth says that if you can do it, it ain't bragging. But we have been told since childhood that talking about our achievements is risky business unless accompanied by suitable self-deprecations. So we bend over backwards to avoid taking credit for the good we do. Being unwilling to brag, meaning to admit graciously that we are talented, is a way of staying a Loser. I slaved over a résumé once; I spent five days drawing up a description of myself that was to be used in finding another job. I proudly took it to some dear friends to critique (meaning they would tell me what a good job I had done.) He read it and handed it to her. She read it and then tore up all four precious pages! I literally screamed, "My God, Betty, what are you doing!" She explained that the résumé described someone else; she liked me too much to let me send that kind of lie to a future employer. We studied what I had done. Without exception I had carefully shown that I was somewhat above the idiot level and had equally de-emphasized most of my good points. My friends then helped me put together a résumé that was accurate and therefore a lot more valuable to me.

People seem to be far more willing to forgive us our failures and our shortcomings than they are to forgive us our successes. "Glad you got it worked out today, Myrtle (but watch out for tomorrow—it ain't anything permanent, you know!)" "Congratulations, Charlie. How in the world did you manage that?" "Oh, yeah? Well, once *I* did the same thing." If we want friends, perhaps we'd better get with the meek and mild routine.

We get stroked for putting out effort with minimal results, for putting up with intolerable situations, for waiting, for searching "everywhere" for an answer, for "trying" to get things right, whether we do or not, and for "sticking it out." Why should we decide to be potent?

It's a small step from non-assertiveness to wasting time and energy by being a doormat. "I just let him walk all over me." The myth is that doormats just lie there. That isn't true. I am convinced that we will all get our "air time," one way or the other. If we don't get our needs met "up front," then we figure a way in through the back door. Mrs. Bopbiddle sits through a meeting and watches something happening that she doesn't like. Except for a few snide, whispered remarks to the mister, she simply sits and glares. An hour after the meeting she is burning up the telephone wires. You'd think she was chairman of the board. She bitches, she puts people down, she complains and scolds. Now it is *her* turn.

Sammy goes to a movie with Sally. He didn't want to see that picture and he didn't want to admit it. He gets even (meaning he gets *his* air time) by pouting and doing a lot of jumping up and down, going to the men's room, to the popcorn stand, and back again to the men's room.

Sally agrees to go with Sam to a football game, which she hates. She gets even by dragging her heels, carefully stalling until amost too late, then hurrying through her bath, having to close and lock doors, tidy up the living room. . . . You know how it works; you may have done something similar.

Getting even *feels* like winning; we experience it sometimes as potency or power. It is none of these. Vengeance, or getting even, is an illusion. While in the process of making the other guy pay, we put ourselves in far worse positions than we were in, and usually have little effect on the person we want to damage. A dry alcoholic reported one of the best things about his change in life patterns: "I no longer have to drive halfway to Dallas just to shoot the bird to some guy who cut in front of me! Revenge is a luxury I can no longer afford."

In the Bible, God is quoted as saying: "Vengeance is mine; I will repay." That's probably how the idea of a fire-and-brimstone hell got started. "Teacher's gonna get you, teacher's gonna get you!" My understanding is that by the very nature of things, we catch our hell while we are looking and feeling "one up." Remember the big bully on the block; how you wanted so much to smash him one? I've never seen a bully that was happy. Their combative behavior is the way they act out their miseries. It also reinforces their miserable feelings. The *grand dame* who is always looking down the end of her nose at folk has neck aches you wouldn't believe! Among other things.

We don't *need* to get even. That's already been settled!

I believe the "meek inherit the earth" and that they are blessed. But not the way it is usually translated. Simply letting people smack you one, physically or verbally, while you stand there looking patient and beatific isn't going to conquer any worlds. Blending in with the woodwork seldom makes people feel blessed.

Meek does not mean "like a doormat." Even Webster defines it as "mild of temper; patient under injuries; long-suffering." The word describes the qualities which come from having your act together. One of my favorite movie scenes is from *Love Is a Many Splendored Thing*. Han Su Yin tells her lover, Mark Elliot, that he is one of the strongest men she has ever met. He is puzzled and asks her how she can say that. "You are the strongest because you are the *gentlest* man I have known." People who go Blap-Blap-Blap through life are not strong. They strike out at people because it's the best way they know, in their weakness, to get things done. People who know they are strong have no need to advertise; their strength will be there when they need it. One of the gentlest people I ever met had a black belt in karate.

The meek are people who have gotten out of their Loser programs and no longer wait for Santa to make their lives neat. They have no need to persecute others—to zap them— in order to feel "one up" themselves. They are no longer at odds with the world and with themselves.

The motto says these people are "blessed," which is theologically described as "the highest stage of happiness and well-being." Now the motto makes sense. The meek are people who are busy being happy and feeling good about themselves and their lives. They are the people who will outlast, and outwin, the Stormers and Stompers and Stabbers. Not to mention the Mousey Folk.

This may come as a surprise to some of you, but there is nothing in the Bible or the Christian Gospel that advocates, or approves of, being a Mouse, a Wimp, a Milktoast, or a Loser. There is nothing that says being a Winner is wrong. Nowhere will you find it scolding people who are capable, effective, happy, put together, and "making it."

The Good Book is about how to get ourselves synchronized with the world, with other people, with nature, with our bodies, and with what we call God. Because it was written by men and women, it sometimes does this through their particular Conceptual Grids (Flat World and all) but the writers were still interested in winning! Jesus used to say a weird thing: "Peace be with you." Peace was something people tried to get *around* them, not with them. That's why he called it the "peace that passes understanding," meaning the kind of peace that doesn't make sense.

Most people can feel peaceful when they are out on a farm. The peace that "doesn't make sense" is the calm we can have in the middle of havoc. We either have it *within us all the time,* or we never have it, even on the farm. This internal quietude comes with *being in charge of our own lives,* with being potent, and with winning. It's the difference between merely feeling peaceful and being at peace.

So how do we get to be "good meek" and avoid "bad meek"? This book has been about the ways we learned to operate ineffectively and what we can do to change them. We have seen the tremendous impact our cultural surroundings have in reinforcing our Froggy Ways. We have looked at some of the mottoes and clichés that helped us get there and found some other translations that might work better. In *No Grown-Ups in Heaven,* I ended the book with eight starter suggestions for becoming more potent. I'd like to add ten more ideas for taking charge of our lives:

1. *List your resources:* If you are going to build a barn, the first thing you need is some wood. Since the wood isn't going to walk over to your house some morning and knock on the door, you need to go find it, usually in lumber yards. There are plenty of resources available; they need to be gathered. Until we have the available materials, we're not going to take action.

Many of you have said, and heard your children say, usually with a whine, "There's nothing to do!" That's easy to say and *never* true. So make a list of "things to do." You may not want to do most of them, but get them on a list anyway so you can quit convincing yourself that you are without resources.

The person who says "I have no one to turn to" is lying. A list of People I *Could* Talk to About My Problem will invariably be a long one.

I envision a Resource List as having many sections. Places To Go, Things To Do, People To See, Books To Read, Ideas To Think About, Things To Learn, and so on. The most important list has to do with resources that lie within us. I frequently have people make a list of What is Good About Me. They struggle first, wanting to respond, "Nothing!" With a little effort, they usually come up with a list of many assets they have. "I can cook, sew, sail a boat; I am friendly, intelligent, industrious, and sincere. I am responsible and trustworthy." We are so accustomed to making lists of What's Wrong With Me that we literally blind ourselves to our internal resources.

I like lists. They often help. One lady, dreading the arrival of her mother (and her mom's criticism) for the Christmas holidays, figured out a way to deal with the nagging. She composed a list of every possible thing her mom might criticize. She came up with hundreds of items. When her parents arrived, one of her mom's first sentences was, "Your tree decorations are dusty!" My friend broke into peals of laughter. When asked why, she produced her list, explained it, and said, "And you picked something that I hadn't thought of." After a short sulk, mom gave up pointing out faults and the families had a great two weeks together. The list helped get that done.

If you're being stubborn about coming up with items for your What is Good About Me list, interview your family and friends. Most of them will be happy to help you add some things you're forgetting.

2. *Review all the options before deciding what "reality" is:* No fair "editing" while you're making the list! One of the hardest things for writers to learn is to separate writing and editing. Most of us write so carefully that after five hours of

work we have only one lousy page done. We decide to give up the project since we "can't write." I find it useful to pour out everything, knowing that I won't use a lot of the stuff. After it's all down on paper, I can go back and do the editing, crossing off the bad stuff, rearranging the rest.

When listing the options, put down everything and evaluate later. Let's say you have a friend who never calls you for lunch. When you call him, you both seem to enjoy the time together. So why doesn't he call you? "He doesn't really like me" is only *one* of the possibilities. He may regard you very highly and tells himself that he has no right to impose on such an important person. His wife may not like you, and she belittles him for liking you, so he waits for you to call. Then he can tell her that he was only being polite. He may have a See How Lonely I Am program going and wants to prove how few friends he has. He may think that if he calls someone for lunch he ought to pay for it, and he doesn't have that much money. And so on. Until we have considered *all* the possibilities, however wild, deciding what the "reality" is can be risky.

If you want to decide how to respond to a "sticky wicket" like that, the same operation is useful. If one of your options is hitting him with a skillet, write it down even though you know you absolutely won't do that. It's an option and will help you understand that you aren't nearly the *helpless* victim you feel.

3. *Understand the other person's frame of reference.* If your problem involves another person, then it helps to understand (and accept) his Conceptual Grid. If he thinks nicknames are insulting, then using his proper name will be far easier and more useful than trying to rearrange his frame of reference. Quit calling him "Pooky!"

Acceptance, by the way, does not imply approval. I neither approve nor disapprove of the Mexican peso. I accept it as the Mexican's frame of reference for exchange. When I am in Mexico I use the peso rather than the dollar. It works well.

That could be a whole brand-new motto. "When in Mexico, do as the Mexicans do."

Knowing how the other guy thinks is of critical importance in communication. When ships communicate with flags they are restricted to the code they have in common. You won't find that common ground unless you are paying attention to how the other person thinks. Marc Gold, an agency trainer, tells of work done with a retarded in-patient. The counselor wanted to give the girl some time by herself to play in the park. She also wanted her to be back in ninety minutes, but the girl wasn't capable of learning to tell time. While playing with a watch, she observed that the girl became very excited when the two hands came together at twelve. Voila! Whenever the girl went off, the counselor would set her wristwatch at 10:30 and instruct the girl to return when the hands came "together at the top." Worked like a charm.

4. *Put things in perspective.* This may take some effort and change on our part to accomplish, since we think we already have the right perspective! An apt story I just heard illustrates my point. A teen-age girl came home from school one day and asked her father with a loud sigh what he would do if she were pregnant. He bounced off the wall a time or two, got composed, and dealt fairly well with the hypothetical situation. When he was through, she announced: I'm not pregnant, dad, but I *am* going to get a C in chemistry. I wanted you to see that in perspective." Some folk treat a C on a six-week report card as if it were a pregnancy. Investing time to find the correct perspective keeps us from killing flies against the walls with a sledgehammer. The investment is more than returned when we discover that we don't have to do so much plastering anymore.

5. *Have all the experiences you safely can have.* Our frame of reference, our options, and our internal resources are directly related to our experience. The more kinds of ex-

periences we have had, the easier it is to deal with life. I've always liked the merit badge approach of the Boy Scout movement. To advance in rank, a boy must learn a lot of different skills. An Eagle Scout has to become proficient in twenty-one *different* areas.

I suspect that many of our feelings of impotence have to do with living through the Age of Specialization. Eye, ear, nose and throat doctors won't mess with "athlete's foot." Someday they will probably specialize in right ears and left ears. We have brickmasons and stonemasons. We derive great benefits from specialists, but a number of folk who are experts in one narrow field can still get lost in a closet. There is something enormously potent-feeling about being able to change your own light switches or build your own picture frames. The more things we know how to do, the more potent and capable we feel, and the less reliant on others for our survival.

A young executive, now quickly "moving up the ladder" in his company, describes his first summer's work after high school. Because of hard times he had taken a job as a lumber-jack's helper in the Oregon woods. It was literally a whole new way of life for him. Nothing was similar to what he had experienced before that, and there was no way out. He refers to that period of time as the most important educational time of his life. At its conclusion he had learned a very important thing—he could handle *anything* that came along.

Similar programs are available today in which people learn that same lesson by camping out, climbing mountains, and going to sea. We are beginning to relearn self-reliance.

I am pleased that the phrases "women's work" and "men's work" are gradually disappearing. A boy who has to wait for some woman to make his bed becomes a Victim. A girl who waits for some man to fix the tire on her bike will feel a little more helpless.

I emphasize *different* experiences. Many people who think

they have forty years' experience in something have actually had one year's experience forty times. That's a big difference.

6. *Identify your childhood no-no's.* During our childhood development we learned there were some things we were absolutely forbidden to do, or be. It seemed at the time a matter of absolute survival. Transactional analysis calls these early decisions Injunctions. Injunctions come in many forms: "Don't ask for what you want." "Don't do anything important." "Don't finish what you start." "Don't be pretty." "Don't be intelligent." "Don't be healthy." "Don't talk back." "Don't tell people what you're feeling." "Don't feel." "Don't be childlike." There are many more.

You can spot an injunctional decision which you made as a little person. First, you will see yourself repeating that type of behavior over and over. You might describe it as "just the way I am." You will see it as very normal behavior for you, and very understandable. You will have a hundred reasons why it has to be.

The second way you can spot an injunction is to become aware of how hard you fight back when someone suggests that you really *aren't* that way, or that you don't have to *stay* that way. These modes of behavior we have are so deeply rooted that we get into a full-blast stubborn attitude when someone messes with them, even if that "someone" is us. We will argue, deny, explain, and if necessary, get very agitated about the whole idea of altering our behavior.

Third, when we come close to breaking an injunction, we will experience a lot of nervous anxiety. Our insides will churn when we are being potent in a forbidden area. People who are not supposed to be successful will get physically upset when they are. "Sickly people" will start worrying when they have to endure an unseemly long attack of good health. Nervous anxiety almost always means we are doing something that our Life Program says is forbidden.

As you identify your childhood no-no's, you can redecide them. What made sense at age four will not necessarily make sense at thirty-four. Perhaps you couldn't successfully talk back to mom and dad; but you *can* respond potently and accurately to those around you today—if the issue is redecided.

7. *Distinguish between persistence and stubbornness.* Are your heels dug in? Are you determined to do what you plan "no matter what the cost"? "No matter what the results"? A healthy persistence always has one eye on the possibility of good results. Hammering a finishing-nail into a piece of furniture takes persistence. It also requires some degree of care as you get close to the surface; otherwise, you will damage the finish. Stubbornness bangs away and never mind the finish. "I'm going to get that dude in if it's the last thing I do!"

8. *When in trouble, list the transactions from start to finish.* We tend to think in shorthand. "I was just talking and then he hit me." Most often there are fourteen intermediate steps that we ignore in our report. If the problem lies in one of those middle steps, we miss how it happened, and end up feeling out of control. A young math teacher explained to me why she makes her students write out every step of a problem, often to their great annoyance. "If you do it in your head, you will not be able to spot any mistakes. You'll make the same mistake the next time and the time after that."

The same thing is true with problem solving. Unless we get the steps clearly before us, we will assume that each one correctly followed the one before, and we will continue to operate in the same way. By analyzing the transactions that lead us into a "bad place," we can (if we want) discover the discounts, the power plays, the lean-ons, the myths, the hidden agendas and other "contaminated areas" that were responsible.

9. *Make sure you have leverage before you proceed.* Dr. Harry Boyd gave me a helpful idea.* He pointed out that to

*Harry Boyd, "Therapeutic Leverage," *TA Journal*, vol. 6:4, pp. 40ff.

accomplish movement we must have leverage—like prying a stone out of the ground with a long crowbar. Harry maintains that in a transaction between two people, the person who wants the most has the least leverage, and therefore is in an impotent position. That's one of those "it's so obvious, why didn't I think of it?" things. If a boy wants to date a girl more than she wants to date him, he discovers that she has all the power. She can decide not only if they go out, but where and when and under what conditions. When buying a car we get leverage when we want the car less than the merchant wants us to have it. He will only reduce the price or throw in some extra goodies if he thinks we will walk away without them.

Remember how powerless you felt when you wanted number two son to pick up his room more than he wanted to? Or when you wanted to go to the ballgame more than your mate? Things work out best when the leverage is equal. But I've learned to quit bouncing up and down when I'm on the short end of the teeter-totter! I love that analogy. I have spent so much time and energy in my life futilely bouncing up and down and wondering why that other stupid end wouldn't budge. You don't have to bounce much before you begin feeling dumb, ineffective, and powerless.

Our kids clean up their rooms when they want to, not when we decide they should. They clean up less frequently than I now think they should, but far more frequently than I did in college. Hmmmmm.

An executive reported having trouble persuading a subordinate to turn in his expense account within a reasonable period. For months he would plead and cajole; in the meantime his books were being fouled up. He turned the leverage around by posting a notice that expense accounts would not be paid if they were more than three months old. After thinking about it, the junior man decided he wanted his money back more than he wanted to piddle around. Problem solved.

10. *Be willing to use sufficient energy to get the job done*

My dad taught me an aphorism I still like: "If it's worth doing at all, it's worth doing well." *Well* means getting the job *done.* Different jobs require different tools, and sometimes the same job requires a tool of a different size.

If you are determined to use a ⅜-inch wrench on a ¾-inch bolt, you might as well work a jigsaw puzzle. Most of us have chosen ways of behaving that "fit well in our hand," and then use only those behaviors in every situation.

What I want to describe is best shown in an analogy. When chiseling out a spot to place a door hinge, I must use as much force in hammering on the chisel as the wood exerts in resisting it. If I use too little energy I will only dent the wood or take a hundred years to finish the job. On the other hand, if I use too much power I will drive the chisel past the right spot, perhaps even destroying the piece of wood I want to reshape.

Most transactional difficulties between people are the result of one or the other error. I've seen parents and supervisors trying, unsuccessfully, to deal with "heavy behavior" by using "light behavior." They are disappointed when the other person fails to respond. I've seen counselors try to deal with suicidal clients by using soft, easy, socially approved approaches. People who wish to kill themselves are exerting *heavy* energies, and only heavy responses have any effect on them. Telling them that you "wish they wouldn't" or that "God won't like it" seldom works, if ever. Same with bank robbers.

Try it some time. Next time you're around a four-year-old who screams in hopes of getting a cookie or something, scream back. Almost every time I've tried it, the child quits crying and gives me a puzzled look. "Why isn't his screaming working?" he wonders. He can be talked with when the screaming stops. Sometimes the kid keeps screaming and I give up, which illustrates my point. I let him "out-potent" me! Momentarily. My next step is either to ignore his scream (he will quit when his throat starts hurting) or put him where I can't hear him. Either way he will decide to quit sooner or later when he discovers that screaming is not a useful way to get what he wants. Same with whining. But you have to be *at least* as potent as the other person.

"Well," you say. "I'm not about to scream back, even in fun!" OK. That's your decision to make. But if you are unwilling to hit a chisel with the required energy, then don't blame God or your parents for the wood not falling out.

The Postlude

Living an OK, abundant life today requires us to examine the guidelines we are using to see if they are still true. Perhaps they never were! If your guidelines are bent, you are free to trade them in for straight ones. There is nothing sacred "in life." Even "sacred cows" aren't sacred. *Life* is what's sacred.

BV
4501.2
.6746
1978

$6.95